To Jo Ann & Dino
With Love —
Joe Gann

THE
TRUTH ABOUT
RHYTHM

by Dr. I. E. Georg

Translated from the German by
Edward Gallagher

P. J. KENEDY & SONS · NEW YORK

THE TRUTH ABOUT RHYTHM
is a translation of *Die Frau und die Ehe*
by Dr. I. E. Georg (Vienna: Verlag Styria,
1961, 8th revised edition)

NIHIL OBSTAT
DANIEL V. FLYNN, J.C.D.
Censor Librorum

IMPRIMATUR
✠ FRANCIS CARDINAL SPELLMAN
Archbishop of New York

New York
July 3, 1962

The nihil obstat and imprimatur are official declarations that a book or pamphlet is free of doctrinal or moral error. No implication is contained therein that those who have granted the nihil obstat and imprimatur agree with the contents, opinions or statements expressed.

Library of Congress Catalogue Card Number: 62–16531
Copyright © 1962 by P. J. Kenedy & Sons, New York
Manufactured in the United States of America

CONTENTS

v

PART TWO
The Practice of Natural Birth Control

Contents

FOREWORD

No work which deals with the problems of marriage can ignore the question of periodic abstinence. This method of practicing such abstinence, which is founded in the main upon the teachings of Dr. Hermann Knaus, the world-famous Viennese professor, provides a natural way of avoiding a source of matrimonial strain.

One still finds numerous prejudices and misunderstandings in many works. Even well-intentioned writers, who strongly support natural methods of birth control, occasionally spread wrong views and cause disappointments for the simple reason that they say too little about the practice of this method of periodic abstinence. Naturally, every book cannot describe the practice of periodic abstinence in the fullest detail, but writers should make it absolutely clear to their readers that a simple formula, a calendar, or a temperature curve, is not sufficient in itself to ensure the success of this method, that much more important is a thorough exposition of the method and of its difficulties.

In this book we have taken particular care to expound the method of periodic abstinence *exactly* and as far as possible in a way which will be easily understood. The practical guidance, which conforms to the current state of scientific knowledge, is given in three ways:

1. *Calculation* of the sterile days, paying special attention to the *personal peculiarities* of the woman.
2. *Determination* of the sterile days through the taking of the *waking temperature*.
3. The *glucose test* to establish the time of ovulation.

In addition to a purely practical purpose, our principal concern is to assist in the understanding of the high moral, personal, and social values which a harmonious relationship between the sexes ensures, as well as the benefit which healthy matrimonial and family life and ordered demographic increase all imply in the preservation and development of our civilization.

DR. I. E. GEORG

PART ONE

THE RHYTHM OF THE
FERTILE AND STERILE DAYS

I

THE ANSWER TO A
MATRIMONIAL PROBLEM

About the year 1930, natural science startled us with important discoveries which provided us with a more profound and accurate knowledge of the biological processes of the human body, and especially those connected with the propagation of the species. To many urgent, difficult, and hitherto unanswered questions posed by married life these discoveries provided a solution which was morally irreproachable and at the same time a notable service and a valuable contribution to public health. The solution deals with the determination of the regular rhythm of fertile and sterile days in a woman's monthly cycle.

During the intervening years science has not stood still. The value of recording body temperatures in order to determine the sterile days was something we learned after World War II; more recently in the United States there was discovered the glucose test which is a valuable aid in assessing the time of ovulation. All this we shall discuss in its proper place.

Knowledge of the periods of fertility and sterility makes it possible—without violating one's conscience or transgressing the natural law—to control conception, and thereby to order married life more perfectly. Science can now place itself at the disposal of the family and the child so that the married state, which has suffered so grievously through the artificial contraceptive practices of the past hundred years, may be established

3

again on foundations sane, natural, and in conformity with human dignity. Not only will many couples be spared grave scruples of conscience and constant anxiety, but the new knowledge, correctly incorporated into the general mode of living and into the framework of marriage, will be a valuable aid in rendering their marriages more harmonious. Further, by eliminating influences damaging to the seminal cells, it makes a positive contribution to the hygiene of procreation. It is, therefore, of tremendous importance to public health. In short, since it benefits both the individual and society in general, it represents an advance of permanent value to civilization.

The present work is designed to tell the reader, as simply as is possible, about this discovery and to show how the method based on it may be safely integrated into normal everyday life. Our aim is a healthy and normal family, and these pages will show how married life, ordered along the lines of these new discoveries, can hold more beauty, happiness, and success and how much less burdensome, with such aids, can be the obligations of the married state.

The new biological discoveries are much more than a mere "method"—they represent a fundamental advance in our knowledge of the natural order of the physiological processes in the male body and the female body, in our knowledge of the law of nature established by God. It would seem incomprehensible that, as certain people seem to fear, a knowledge of these natural laws, ordained by God, should result in the destruction of the Christian family. It would be strange indeed if the creative work of God must be passed over in silence out of fear of endangering the moral law. The sterile days, after all, do not owe their origin to either Knaus [1] or Ogino [2] but to the Creator.

[1] Professor Hermann Knaus was born on October 19, 1892, at Sankt Veit an der Glan, Austria. A scientist and clinician, he explored the mysteries of human propagation. His teaching on the rhythmical alternation of fertility and sterility in women is of fundamental importance to married life for all future generations.
[2] Dr. Kyusaku Ogino is a Japanese gynecologist of Niigata who, independently and at almost the same time, reached conclusions similar to those of Knaus.

The use of the word "method" tends to obscure this fact.

Let us place our trust in Providence. If the natural order, which was not understood by seekers after truth until the twentieth century, is in conformity with eternal Wisdom, then man may acquaint himself with it and accept its principles with respect provided that he submits, with equal reverence, to the moral laws of God.

This new knowledge represents a permanent advance, and experience teaches us that progress cannot be halted. Whether or not this new advance is a good or a bad thing or whether it may not be abused, is not the question. Our purpose is to show how this advance may be incorporated into a general pattern of life, so that it may be beneficial and used with a minimum of abuse. It is how to do this that we shall try to explain in all good faith.

II

THE PHYSIOLOGICAL PROCESSES
OF THE FEMALE BODY

1. The periodic rhythm of the physiological functions

a) Ovaries and female hormones

In the sexual act two individual human beings are united in the closest possible bond that can be achieved by nature. This intimate union affects the couple psychologically as well as physically and so the two prerequisites, mind and body, are of equal importance. Intimately bound together, they achieve a common result. If either prerequisite is missing, the sexual act will be impossible or unnatural.

It is evident, then, that any description of the physiological processes involved in the sexual life would be incomplete unless the psychological factor receives equal attention (and this factor we shall consider in Part Three of this book). In this section we shall describe the bodily processes from a particular point of view: the achievement of fertilization.

Everything that we would call "feminine" in a woman results from the collective action of several different glands, which send their secretions, called hormones, into the blood stream. The glands that are most important for female sexuality are two small ones called ovaries, which are attached to the wall of

6

the abdominal cavity. Their presence is essential to the fertility of a woman and they also determine the appearance of the external signs of female sexuality, for the substances (hormones) which the ovaries send into the blood stream are responsible for developing the feminine characteristics—the graceful body, the typical hair growth, the tone of the voice, and all the other conspicuous physical attributes which are, more or less, peculiar to women.

The course of life of the normal woman is characterized by the periodic rhythm of her bodily functions, of which the most distinguishing feature is the menstrual period, which occurs every month and which has strong repercussions on the psychological life of the woman.

The primary task of the ovaries is the formation of the ovum. This function is designed to ensure the propagation of the human species, for the ovum represents the maternal contribution to the procreation of a child.

Every month, or, to be more precise, in the course of every monthly cycle, an ovum comes to maturity in one of the two ovaries, often right and left alternately. If it is not fertilized, the cycle ends with menstruation and a new ovum matures during the next cycle. This continual succession of ovulation and menstruation, normally interrupted only by pregnancy—that is, only by the gradual formation of a new human being—will endure throughout the greater part of a woman's life, from maidenhood to the threshold of old age.

Let us take a closer look at what takes place in the course of such a cycle.

b) Maturation and ovulation

The ovaries are located in the pelvic cavity, one on each side of the uterus. They have the size and shape of an almond, that is, they are oblong and measure about 1 inch to 1¾ inches in length and about ¼ inch to ¾ inch in width.

The tissue of the ovaries forms a large number of undeveloped ova (primary follicles), or unripe ova as one might call them, only a very few of which may reach fruition in the course of a woman's life.

At the very beginning of the cycle, even during menstruation, a vesicle starts to form in one of the ovaries and grows rapidly. This is called a follicle, or ovisac, because it contains an ovum in the process of maturing. This egg cell is surrounded by other cells which nourish and protect it. It continues thus and, within a few days, reaches the size of a hazelnut and is filled with a colorless fluid.

As the follicle matures, the connection between the ovum and the cells which surround it becomes correspondingly less. In the follicle itself, however, the ovum does not free itself completely from the cells which feed it.

When fully matured, the follicle bursts, and the ovum, with its adhering cells, is carried into the abdominal cavity. This expulsion of the ovum from the follicle constitutes the most important happening in the course of the cycle and, from the Latin word for egg, *ovum*, is commonly known as ovulation.

The released ovum measures only about $\frac{1}{120}$ inch, and so is barely visible. It has now taken the first step on its way toward becoming an organic cell of greater size. The next stage of evolution, the second maturation division, must be accomplished within the space of a few hours, otherwise the ovum will die; but the ovum is incapable of achieving this second stage unaided—it must have the assistance of a male seminal cell, the spermatozoon. If the ovum fails to make contact with this, it cannot survive.

In any event, whether or not it has been fertilized, the ovum, having left the follicle, continues its journey to the uterus. Each of the two ovaries is surrounded by the downy, funnel-shaped extremities of what are known as the Fallopian tubes, and one of these tubes receives the fluid flowing out of the burst follicle and the ovum borne along by it. The ovum then makes its way through a canal about five inches in length, the oviduct, and arrives in the uterus after about four days.

What has become of the follicle in the meantime?

c) *The yellow body and its hormone*

Once the ovum has been expelled, the follicle undergoes changes. Another vesicle is formed, called, because of its color, a yellow body or, in the Latin, the *corpus luteum*. In this yellow body is produced a new hormone which is essential for the final stage of the cycle, and whose greatest influence is exerted on the womb. It is called Progesterone.

This hormone acts also on the ovaries themselves. It prevents a new follicle from maturing. But, while it retards the work of the ovaries, it stimulates the development of the breasts. Under its influence the tissues of the mammary glands develop and swell, causing a feeling of tightness and an increase in sensitivity. In a later section we shall study the effect produced by the yellow body's hormone on the bodily temperature of a woman.

The yellow body attains the culminating point in its development nine days after ovulation. If the ovum has not been fertilized, that is, if there has been no conception, then, on the tenth day, the yellow body starts to wither and degenerate; on the thirteenth day its hormone activity comes to a complete stop—that is, it no longer sends any secretions into the blood stream. As a result, one day later menstruation begins.

The usual interval between ovulation and the next menstruation is 14 days; in other words, the last ovulation takes place on the 15th day before the start of menstruation. Slight variations are always possible, even among healthy women.

One of the great achievements of Professor Knaus, resulting from patient research, was the discovery that the normal time for ovulation to occur is on the 15th day before the next menstruation. As slight variations are possible, in general practice (especially when the most favorable time for conception is being determined), ovulation is regarded as taking place between the 14th and 16th day before the beginning of the next menstrual period.

On the other hand, when it is the sterile days that are being calculated, the method of the Japanese gynecologist, Dr. Ogino, is generally followed, and the ovulation period is placed between the 12th and 16th day before the start of the next menstruation. This is also the practice which we have followed, but we shall revert to this matter later.

It is extremely important to remember that the ovulation period is reckoned by counting the days backward from the start of the next menstruation. It is also possible to determine the ovulation period directly, as we shall see further on.

Why does menstruation occur when the yellow body ceases to function?

d) The uterus and menstruation

When the ovum is released from the follicle, and a yellow body has been formed which discharges its secretion (hormones) into the blood stream, these secretions also travel to the uterus. This is a hollow, pear-shaped muscular organ, about 3½ inches long and 2 inches wide, attached to the vagina by a narrow neck. As we know, the oviducts end at the other side of the uterus. The inner wall of the uterus is coated with a mucous membrane which, under the influence of the hormones of the ovary, begins to increase in size and to proliferate; it swells, extends, thickens, and forms numerous glands. In this way the uterus carries out all the necessary preparations for the reception of a fertilized ovum which arrives by way of the oviduct, and is able to provide it with all the nutritive elements required for its further growth and development. The uterine mucous membrane makes this preparation for the reception of a fertilized ovum in every cycle, irrespective of whether or not fertilization has taken place.

The tissue of the uterine mucous membrane reaches the culminating point in its development on the same day as does the yellow body, that is, on the 9th day after ovulation, and, therefore, on the 6th day before menstruation. When no fertilized ovum reaches the uterus, the mucous membrane ceases its development on the 10th day after ovulation, that is, on the 5th day before menstruation. On the 14th day after the release of the ovum, when the yellow body has degenerated, the mucous membrane starts to detach itself from the wall of the uterus, causing tears and consequent hemorrhages. The blood flows, carrying with it the detached shreds of mucous membrane, and menstruation begins.

The yellow body's hormone has a direct and sedative influence on the uterine muscle which has become stretched, slack, and inert, but, as soon as the action of the yellow body hormone ceases, the muscle becomes taut again and begins to contract.

Menstruation usually ceases after four or five days; the uterine mucous membrane awaits the action of the hormones of a fresh follicle.

The unfertilized ovum, which arrives in the womb through the oviduct, is not able to cling to the uterine mucous membrane; it is already dead. It wends its way to the neck of the uterus, through which, too tiny to be visible, it disappears—at the latest—at the start of menstruation.

e) The course of the cycle

Professor Knaus has tried to explain the normal course of the cycle through the medium of a diagrammatic sketch (see Fig. 1). The plan shows the evolution of the cycle, from one day to the next, side by side, and moving from left to right.

The first day of menstrual bleeding is counted as the first day of the cycle. As we have already said, during and after menstruation a follicle is forming in the ovary, in which an ovum is beginning to ripen. The follicle also sends a secretion into the blood stream, the follicular or estrogenic hormones.

How long does a follicle take to reach maturity; that is, how much time elapses between the start of menstruation and the liberation of the ovum, or ovulation? It is surprising and extremely remarkable that this period, which is called the follicular phase, is never constant; it not merely varies from woman

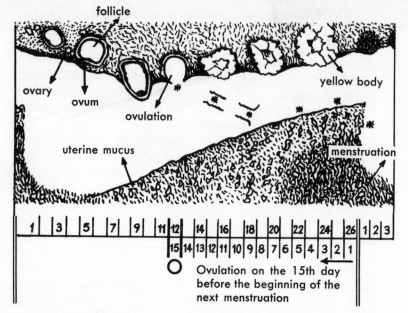

Ovulation on the 15th day
before the beginning of the
next menstruation

Fig. 1. Cycle of 26 days. Schematic representation of the changes which occur in the ovary, in the unfertilized ovum, and in the uterine mucous membrane in the course of the cycle (according to Professor Knaus)

to woman, but it varies from one cycle to the next in the same woman. And on this fluctuation of the follicular phase chiefly depends the duration of the entire cycle up to the next menstruation.

Speaking in very general and statistical terms, one could say that the duration of the follicular phase in healthy women varies between 7 and 20 days, but is usually within the limits of from 10 to 17 days.

In the case of each individual healthy woman the variation is generally not so great; the margin works out at roughly 5 days. We shall deal with this more fully in Chapter IV.

At the end of the follicular phase—more or less in the middle of the cycle—ovulation, the release of an ovum, takes place. It is only then that fertilization is possible, for this is the only time that a living ovum is present. It is, therefore, extremely important to determine the exact time of ovulation.

A new phase of the cycle commences after ovulation, the yellow body phase. We know that the duration of this is usually 14 days. Allowing for some slight variation, its duration is uniform in every healthy woman. Figure 2 illustrates graphically the complete female cycle.

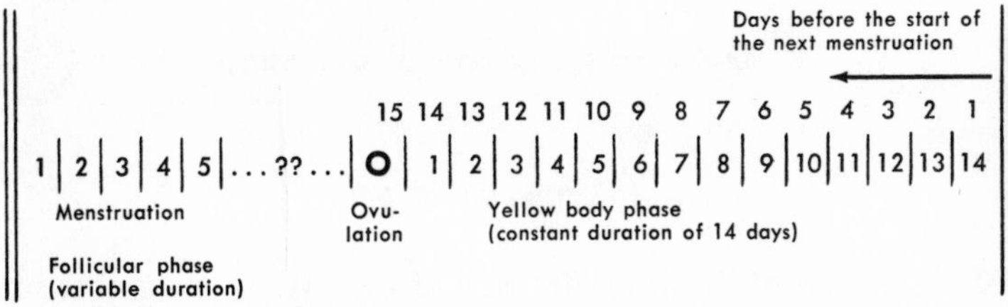

Fig. 2

It can happen indeed that the cycle does not follow a normal course—for instance, that no ovulation takes place. This can occur in the case of young girls at the age of puberty, in older women in the climacteric years, or in nursing mothers. Health upsets can also halt ovulation. In these cases, toward the end of the cycle, there generally occurs false menstruation, known as pseudomenstruation.

On the other hand, the effect of disease can be that menstruation does not occur, either for a temporary period or permanently, although ovulation takes place regularly. Even in such cycles conception is possible.

Furthermore, it can happen that, in comparison with the normal rhythm of a particular woman, her ovulation or menstruation period may vary and be either early or late. Women who have irregular cycles due to health upsets should, of course, seek medical treatment, especially if the troubles are frequent or continuous.

In a healthy woman of child-bearing years, ovulation usually takes place between the 12th and 16th day (most probably on the 15th), before the start of the next menstruation. Consequently, conception is impossible during the last 11 days of the cycle.

In order to find the fertile and sterile days, it is of the greatest importance to determine as exactly as possible and before the cycle ends, the time of ovulation of the woman in question. To do this, we may calculate the ovulation period of the woman in question in advance—we shall speak of this later—or we may observe the symptoms during ovulation.

2. Outward symptoms of ovulation

a) Intermenstrual pain

At the period of ovulation (release of the ovum), a number of women notice certain symptoms, arising from the changes taking place in their bodies. These ovulation symptoms vary from one woman to another. We will describe the signs most frequently encountered.

About two weeks before the coming menstruation many women experience the middle or intermenstrual pain, so called because it usually occurs about the middle of the cycle. This generally takes the form of griping or tension in the lower abdomen. Other women have a feeling of discomfort like the sensation which precedes menstruation. Sometimes this intermenstrual pain is quite severe, but mostly it is only slight and the woman often does not notice it unless she is told to be on the lookout for it. It often disappears after a few hours, but reappears a day or two later. Many women will recognize this pain despite the fact that they have been unaware of it previously. They need only begin to watch for it, and soon they will be able to detect it.

On the other hand, one must be sure that it really is the natural pain related to the process of ovulation that is noted, and that pains of a different nature are not mistaken for the intermenstrual pain. Certainty can be assured if, over a period, the date of the pain experienced is noted and the days from this to the onset of menstruation counted, to see if the pain has occurred 14 or 15 days before menstruation.

The intermenstrual pain may begin one or two days before ovulation. It ceases as soon as the follicle bursts.

Figure 3 is a table of intermenstrual pain, observed over a period of one year, according to Smulders.[1]

Ovulation pain	1st day of menstruation	No. of days from onset of last menstruation to ovulation pain	No. of days from ovulation pain to following menstruation	Duration of cycle
May 27/28, 1933	May 16/17, 1933	11/12	15/14	25/26
June 23	June 11	12	14	26
July 19	July 7	12	14	26
Aug. 13?	Aug. 2	11?	16?	27
Sept. 11	Aug. 29	13	15	28
Oct. 10	Sept. 26	14	15	29
Nov. 8/10	Oct. 25	16	16	32
Dec. 10	Nov. 26	14	15	29
Jan. 7, 1934	Dec. 25	13	14	27
Feb. 3	Jan. 21, 1934	13	14	27
Feb. 27/28	Feb. 17	11	16	27
Mar. 28	Mar. 16	12	11	23
Apr. 23	Apr. 8	15	15	30
May 23/24	May 8	16	14	30
June 20	June 7	13	15	28

Fig. 3

b) *The temperature curve*

In recent times the temperature curve has assumed a role of great importance in determining the time of ovulation.

Specialists have known since the start of the century that there is a regular variation in the bodily temperature of a woman during the monthly cycle, but it was not until recently that from this regular variation in temperature inferences were drawn concerning a woman's periodic fertility.

Among the most valuable researches on this question are those of Professor Raoul Palmer, head of the gynecology department in the Faculty of Medicine, Paris. In his work "Ex-

[1] J. N. Smulders, Dutch physician and philanthropist who died in 1939. His work will be discussed later.

*plorations fonctionnelles échelonnées et convergentes et diag-
nostic hormonal dans la stérilité,"* [2] he gives the following summary (p. 8):

At the same hour every morning, before getting up (7 o'clock, for
preference), the rectal temperature must be taken very accurately
with the same thermometer, and this must be continued for at least
two cycles.

In a normal woman, the morning rectal temperature is around
98.2° on the days following menstruation, drops to about 97.8° during the two or three days' duration of the oestrus, then, as soon as
the yellow body starts to act, climbs again rapidly to 98.8° or 99°,
and remains at a level above 98.6° for the duration of the yellow
body's activity; the temperature falls to 98.6° on the eve of menstruation and remains variable throughout this period.

As Palmer points out elsewhere, the bursting of the follicle
(ovulation) has taken place on the last day of low temperature
(97.8°), in all cases at least 36 hours before the point at which
the temperature climbs again above 98.6°.

Palmer gives a more detailed study of this question in *Les
Tests de l'Ovulation chez la Femme*,[3] which contains a good
bibliography especially of the results of American research on
this subject.

In the *Journal of the American Medical Association* of May
6, 1944, Kleitman recommends taking the temperature by
mouth, and maintains that the results are just as accurate as
those by the rectal method. According to him, the temperature
should be taken at night before retiring. Prior to doing so, the
woman should rest in an armchair for an hour and should
drink no liquids, hot or cold, for half an hour before taking her
temperature. The writer says it is still more satisfactory if the
temperature is taken both morning and evening.

Other European doctors have confirmed Professor Palmer's
findings. Among them are Knaus, Stecher, Holt and Clavero
Núñez.

[2] *Revue française de gynécologie et d'obstétrique*, Sept.-Oct., 1941
[3] Extract from 10e *Congrès Français de Gynécologie*, Lyons, 1946.

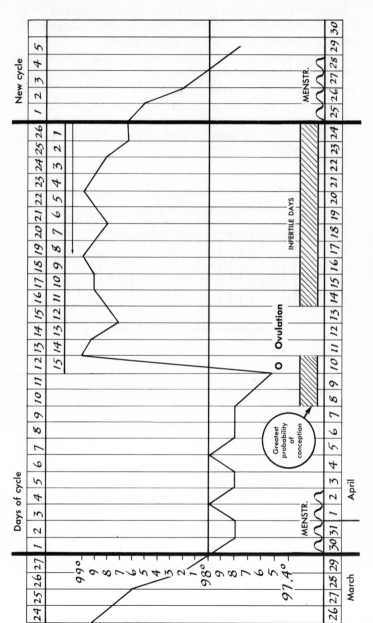

Fig. 4. Temperature chart of a cycle of 26 days

Some doctors recommend inserting the thermometer in the vagina to record the temperature on awakening. Naturally, the temperature is not taken during menstruation.

It is important *always to follow the same method* for taking the temperature. The readings should be recorded at once in the form of a table or graph. Figure 4 is an example of a temperature chart of a cycle of 26 days.

When, for whatever reason, ovulation does not take place, there is no rise of temperature at the time of the expected ovulation (see Fig. 5).

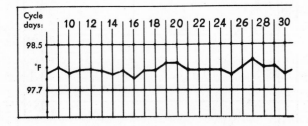

Fig. 5.   Temperature curve of a cycle without ovulation

It is now possible to get special thermometers which facilitate accurate temperature reading. The Ovulindex thermometer (manufactured by Linacre Laboratories, New York 17, N.Y.) is available in most United States drugstores. It is graduated in 0.1° and covers the range 96° to 100°, thus making it easy to read. With it is a handbook to help obtain useful and accurate readings.

c) The sugar content of the uterine mucus

During the days around ovulation, an increased quantity of mucus is secreted at the entrance, or neck (cervix), of the uterus. This is called "cervical mucus." The strongest secretion takes place between the 19th and 14th days *before the onset* of the next menstruation (see Fig. 6).

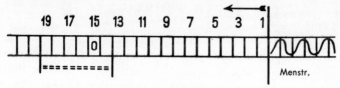

Fig. 6

The mucus is obviously intended to assist sperm penetration. Chemical analysis of uterine mucus has shown that, on the days of ovulation, this contains a significant quantity of glucose, whereas, on the other days of the cycle, there is no trace of it in the uterine mucus of normal women. Since diabetic women have an excess of glucose in the blood, a sugar analysis of the cervical mucus could in their case, of course, produce erroneous findings.

There are two causes for the presence of sugar in the uterine mucus at the time of ovulation: first, glucose is formed by the dissolution of the mucus itself (through the so-called hydrolytic splitting up of glycogen, or liver starch, which is present in the human body);[4] second, sugar in the mucus comes directly from the follicular fluid which, by way of the oviduct, accompanies the ovum, released at ovulation, to the uterus.[5] The purpose of the glucose, provided by the follicular fluid, is probably to give nourishment to the ovum on its way to the uterus.

This glucose, which is formed by the dissolution of the cervical mucus, can already be detected one or two days before ovulation, but this demands care and technical knowledge, for it is present in only very small quantities. On the other hand, as soon as the follicular fluid itself (after ovulation) reaches the neck of the uterus, it is comparatively simple to clearly detect the presence of glucose. The only method is to use a chemically sensitized test paper (reagent paper, colorimetrical test paper), such as "Tes-Tape" manufactured by Eli Lilly & Co., Indianapolis, Indiana. This test paper turns a clear green color under the influence of dissolved glucose.

[4] See Birnberg, *Journal of the American Medical Association*, March 8, 1958.
[5] See Doyle, *Journal of the American Medical Association*, July 19, 1958.

On the last two days before ovulation (that is, on the 16th and 17th day before the next menstruation), the paper assumes only a very pale tinge of green, and sometimes as much as thirty minutes are required before this is discernible. On the day of ovulation itself, however, the paper becomes, more or less rapidly and at the most within five minutes, a deep green. On the two days following ovulation, the green color is again barely discernible, and then only after a fairly long test. On the other days in the cycle of a normal healthy woman, the test paper shows no change of color. (See Fig. 7.)

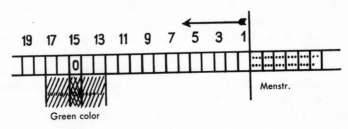

Fig. 7

We shall explain in Chapters IV, §5 and VI, §4 c how this glucose test, with the aid of test papers, can be put to practical use to determine the fertile and sterile days in the cycle.[6]

d) Other ovulation symptoms

Some women are able to detect the stronger mucous excretion of which we spoke in a preceding paragraph by means of a light, vitreous, clear discharge from the vagina. The discharge appears from three to five days before ovulation, and disappears

[6] The colorimetrical process in Tes-Tape paper is based on the effect of specific enzymes (Comer, *Anal. Chem.*, Nov., 1956). Naturally, there are on the market other papers to help detect the presence of glucose—Clinistix, for example, made by the Ames Company. They are sold complete with a description of the color reaction in each case. (As there are several different types manufactured, the color reaction is not always green.)

one or two days afterward. Some women mistake this excretion for vaginal catarrh.

In other cases, slight bleedings occur. These "ovulation bleedings" should not be confused with the flow of blood that takes place at menstruation.

After ovulation most women notice a swelling and tenseness in the breasts. This symptom is caused by the yellow body hormones and disappears as soon as the next menstruation starts.

During the ovulation days many women experience changes in their psychological and sexual sensitivity.

Every woman should pay attention to all these symptoms, and record them carefully in her menstruation calendar.

3. The fertile period

Sexual intercourse at the time of ovulation, or immediately before, is highly likely to result in a fertilization, in the creation of a new life, because then the male spermatozoon can encounter in the oviduct a newly released ovum.

a) The spermatozoa

During sexual intercourse several hundred million spermatozoa are ejaculated by the male into the female body. They are formed in the testicles, the masculine sexual glands. They are extraordinarily tiny, measuring about $\frac{1}{100}$ inch, and are not visible to the naked eye. Each spermatozoon has a long, threadlike tail, the whipping movements of which push it along. Even before they are fully mature, the young spermatozoa have the power of self-locomotion, and from the egg-shaped testicles they move to the epididymis, at the base of the scrotum, where the temperature is about four degrees below the normal body temperature. As a consequence of this cool temperature, the spermatozoa come to rest, without, however, suffering any loss in their reproductive powers which, on the contrary, come to maturity here.

Before being ejaculated by the man at the time of sexual intercourse, the spermatozoa are mixed with secretions from other glands in the male body—from the prostate gland, for example—which increase their motility. The effect of the higher temperature in the female body is to endow the spermatozoa with greater activity, and they press through the uterus into the oviduct. The fluid from the burst follicle acts as a guide. All this traveling causes the spermatozoa to lose their vitality by degrees. After about 30 hours their powers of fertility are probably exhausted though they remain mobile for a little longer.

So that conception may follow, therefore, sexual intercourse must take place on the day of ovulation, or a day or two beforehand, because the spermatozoon does not remain fertile in the female organ beyond this period.

b) The fertilized ovum

When the spermatozoon comes into contact with a newly released ovum traveling to the uterus by way of the oviduct, it penetrates and fuses with it; the second maturation division occurs, fertilization has taken place, and a new being has come into existence. The spermatozoon transmits the paternal hereditary traits, the ovum, the maternal. The human life which has begun will have the protection of the maternal womb.

The fertilized ovum continues its journey through the oviduct to the uterus, where it arrives on the 4th day after ovulation. The growth of the new being continues. Between the 7th and 9th days it is invading the lining membrane of the uterus and even begins to send out new secretions, which the blood stream conveys to the yellow body. Under the influence of these, the yellow body does not degenerate but continues to transmit its hormone to the blood stream, in order to prevent menstruation taking place. Three months pass before the work of the yellow body is completed; after that its activity ceases and it wastes away. By that time the whole female organism has adapted itself to the new living creature in the maternal womb; all the organs collaborate to maintain and stimulate its development up to the moment of birth, which usually follows 272 days after conception.

As we mentioned previously, the yellow body's hormone induces a rise in the temperature of the woman immediately after ovulation. When conception takes place, that rise in temperature continues throughout the first three months. This makes it easy to establish pregnancy at a very early stage, especially if the woman has been reading and recording her temperature regularly. (See Fig. 8.)

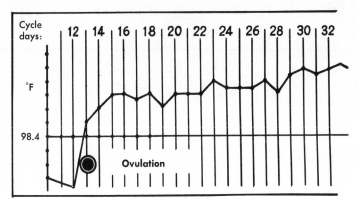

Fig. 8. The temperature curve at the start of pregnancy: the rise in temperature lasts longer than in a normal cycle. Pregnancy already can be established with certainty about 20 days after ovulation

Figure 9 shows the successive changes—they are pictured side by side and read from left to right—in the female body resulting in pregnancy. The illustration becomes clearer if several successive and differing cycles are taken, rather than one alone. Figure 10 shows, firstly, a cycle of 25 days, followed by two successive cycles of 27 days each, and, finally, a fourth cycle

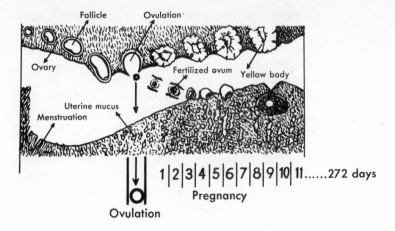

1|2|3|4|5|6|7|8|9|10| 11......272 days

Pregnancy

Ovulation

Fig. 9

which would probably have had a duration of about 29 days, if conception had not occurred around the 14th day.

On what days can conception occur?

4. The fertile and sterile days in women

The number of days elapsing between the start of one menstruation and the start of the next is called the cycle (monthly cycle) of a woman.

The duration of the cycle is calculated by the exact number of days in the following manner: the first day when bleeding starts is, obviously, also the first day of the cycle. The last day, which precedes the onset of the next menstruation, is the last day of the cycle. The first day of the next menstruation does not, therefore, belong to the preceding cycle.

If, for instance, the bleeding starts on the 31st day, the cycle has lasted 30 days, because the 31st day forms part of the next cycle, being the first day of the new cycle.

Important conclusions emerge from what has been said in the preceding paragraph:

The last 11 days of the cycle are *sterile* for most women, for

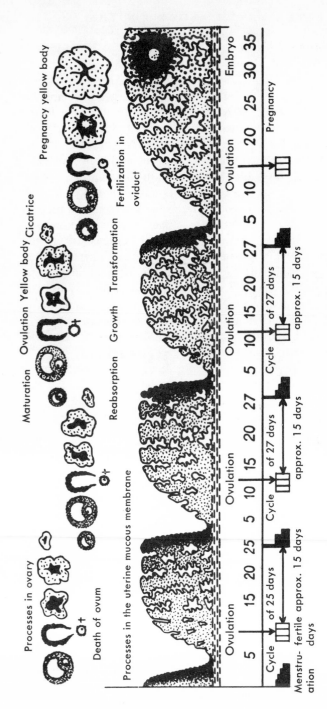

Fig. 10. Diagrammatic sketch of cyclical transformations in the ovary and in the uterine mucous membrane in the course of several cycles; finally, pregnancy (Hornstein-Faller, *Gesundes Geschlechtsleben*, Walter-Olten und Freiburg im Breisgau, 1955)

during this period there is no longer present an ovum capable of being fertilized.

As far as the female organism is concerned, fertilization (pregnancy) is possible only when the follicle bursts, and the ovum leaves the ovary to pass into the oviduct. We do not know the exact date when this takes place, but we do know with certainty that it occurs *between the 12th and the 16th day* preceding the next menstruation. The presence of a fertile ovum is only possible on one of these 5 days in the month.

As the spermatozoon can retain its fertilizing power for only about 2 days in the female body, sexual intercourse must take place on the day of ovulation or at most two days beforehand.

As this calculation takes into account complete days only, and not hours, it is not sufficiently accurate—7 days of abstention are not sufficient to guarantee that conception will not occur. A further day of abstinence must be added. This is all the more essential because of the fact that as the duration of the cycle is calculated in days, not in hours, there may be a difference of half a day or more. The allowance of the extra day provides security against an unwanted conception.

Consequently, a cycle of whose duration we have an exact knowledge has 8 *fertile days*, being the period between the *12th and 19th day* before the next menstruation.

The sterile days are (1) the last 11 days before the next menstruation; and (2) the days which precede the 19th day before the coming menstruation, that is, the 20th, 21st, 22nd, etc., before the next menstruation.

The fertile and sterile days can be reckoned only by counting backward from the first day of the coming menstruation. Figure 11 may help to explain this.

It can be seen from this plan that the last 11 days before menstruation are sterile; the 8 days which precede them (12th to 19th before menstruation) are fertile. The remaining days, counting back from the 20th, are sterile. How many of these are there? This depends on how long the cycle of the woman in question lies. We could not show in the illustration the precise number of days and therefore had to use question marks,

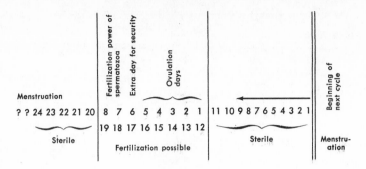

Fig. 11

as the number of days remaining varies with each woman and in each cycle. In a cycle of 30 days, for example, the first 11 days are sterile. If menstruation lasts 4 days (and these are equally sterile), 7 clear days remain after menstruation (see Fig. 12).

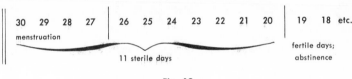

Fig. 12

Figure 13 shows clearly how the number of sterile days at the start of individual cycles differs, according to the length of the cycle in question. In the longer cycles, the number of sterile days in the follicular phase is greater, in the shorter cycles it is less. (The sterile days are represented by the white areas.)

The data thus established form the theoretical basis of the practical method, but are not yet sufficient to ensure its effective application. We must first see how one determines the sterile days, taking into account the variable duration of a cycle from one month to the next. In addition, there are still various other factors to be considered before putting the method into practice. For this reason we shall devote a special chapter to its practical application, and anyone wishing to use the method

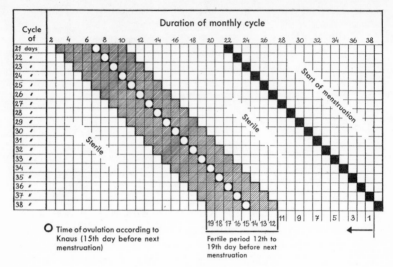

Fig. 13

successfully must study this chapter carefully and follow exactly the instructions given therein. (See Part Two.)

5. New method of natural birth control

Since olden times it has been known that a woman was not fertile on every day of her monthly cycle, but for centuries it was impossible to determine accurately the days when conception was possible, and the days when it was definitely impossible. Various superstitions existed, of course, as they still do, and the most widespread and popular of these held that the period most propitious for conception was on the days preceding, and following menstruation, which has been proved to be completely false.

More than a hundred years ago, in 1842, Pouchet, a French scientist, was the first who sought to clarify the question. He provided a really valuable insight into the biological processes in the female body during the menstrual cycle, but found no definite answer to the problem.[7]

[7] Pouchet, *Théorie positive de l'ovulation spontanée et de la fécondation des mammifères et de l'espèce humaine basée sur l'observation de toute la serie animale*, Paris: J.-B. Ballière, 1842.

Later, in 1883, Dr. Capellmann,[8] a German physician, sought to determine the fertile and the sterile days on the basis of numerous observations. He maintained that a woman was fertile for the first 17 or 18 days of the cycle; she was then sterile for about one week, and became fertile once more 3 *or 4 days before menstruation*. Although this theory proved incorrect, it accidentally tallied with the sterility period of many women. The French scientists, Ancel and Bouin, came nearer the truth.

It is remarkable that scientific researchers after Pouchet should have taken such a long time to arrive at the correct answer. This was due principally to three major mistakes made by most of the investigators which rendered it impossible to discover earlier the natural laws governing the alternation of fertile and sterile days.

1. For a long time there was complete ignorance about the nature of the menstrual cycle. From a study of the behavior of animals, it was found that the sexual urge recurred regularly at definite periods and that it manifested itself by various external signs. During this so-called rutting period, the animals mate, and only during these days are they fertile. It was deduced from this that menstruation, a regular and recurrent period, was synonymous with animal rutting and that, consequently, a woman was most fertile during the time of menstruation. It was known that ovulation (release of the ovum) must, of necessity, precede fertility. As it had been discovered that ovulation took place in animals at the rutting period, it was wrongly assumed from this that ovulation also occurred among women at the menstruation period and that the woman remained fertile as long as the ovum lived. Many maintained that a woman was least fertile exactly in the middle period between one menstruation and the next. All these views are absolutely incorrect, and we mention them only because they are frequently put forward even today.

2. More precise scientific study, at the beginning of the twen-

[8] Capellmann: *Fakultative Sterilität ohne Verletzung der Sittengesetze* (Aachen, 1883, 1895). Capellmann-Bergmann: *Pastoralmedizin* (Bonifazius-Druckerei, Paderborn, 1923).

tieth century, proved that ovulation does not occur at the time of menstruation but, on the contrary, during the time between one menstruation and the next. Nevertheless, because of another grave error in their calculations, scientists were still not success-ful in determining the fertile and sterile phases. They were con-tinually seeking to discover on what day *after the last menstrua-tion* ovulation took place, and their findings were not merely different but contradictory. One considered ovulation as occur-ring on the 6th day, another on the 8th or on the 10th, others on the 15th or the 19th day, etc. It was held from this that the sterile days could not be reckoned in advance from the men-struation dates. This also was a mistake.

3. This seemingly very complicated problem would have been solved much sooner had not a third grave mistake been made in the investigations. It used to be generally assumed that the regular duration of the menstrual cycle was 28 days, and it was believed that the 28-day cycle, the most frequently occurring, was the "normal cycle." (See Chapter III, §2 b.)

Dr. Ogino found as the result of accurate observations that more than 99 per cent of women have nothing like a regular cycle, but that with all women the cycles vary by a few days each way. In addition, he made another very important dis-covery, that is, that even in healthy women a regular cycle of four weeks does not exist; that some have a short cycle of about three weeks, others again have a cycle of from five to six weeks, and that between these two extremes are to be found all sorts of variations.

Ogino began to wonder whether, in women with a short cycle, ovulation did not take place at a time different from those with a long cycle. Then came the surprising discovery which threw light upon the whole question—he found that in all women ovulation always occurs from 12 to 16 days before the next menstruation irrespective of the duration of the cycle. It naturally follows from this that in women with short cycles ovulation can occur as early as the sixth day after the last men-struation, whereas in those with long cycles, it does not take place until the 15th or 20th day. Had the investigators before

Ogino, in their observations of the ovulation period, taken cognizance of the length of the cycles, they would probably have solved the problem long ago. Ogino re-examined the findings of these other scientists which had provided such widely divergent ovulation times, and found that in these cases also ovulation always took place from 12 to 16 days before the next menstruation. The other scientists had not noticed this simply because they had always counted the days from the last menstruation.

Ogino first published his discoveries in Japanese technical journals in 1923. He published them in Europe in 1930, first in Germany. Since then they have been tested frequently and have always proved correct.

Almost at the same time and quite independently of Ogino, Dr. Knaus had evolved a scientific method, the so-called Knaus Test, for determining experimentally the time of ovulation. His conclusions generally were in accord with Ogino's findings. Knaus had the further distinction of throwing valuable scientific light on the processes in the feminine body during the cycle. He also solved the question of how long the spermatozoa retained their fertilization power in the female body. Knaus is without dispute the greatest authority of the day on matters connected with the science of human propagation.

Both Knaus and Ogino put forward the view that the ovum released from the ovary was capable of being fertilized during a quite short period only, a fact confirmed by other important scientists. Besides Knaus, American research workers especially have earned great credit in the solution of this question.

As the result of the conclusions reached on the time of ovulation, the fertility of the ovum and of the spermatozoon, light was thrown upon those laws of nature which had to be known for the determination of the fertile and sterile days in women. The next task was to devise a practical method, an instruction—based on scientific findings and taking into account the differing cycle lengths and variations—as to how conception could be avoided by periodic sexual abstinence. Dr. J. N. Smulders, mentioned earlier, was the first to distinguish himself in connection with this question. He was the first to spread the fame of Ogino and Knaus, and he showed how their doctrine could be put to sure and practical use. All subsequent adaptations of the method have been based on his practical instructions.

6. Knaus or Ogino?

The determination of the fertile and sterile days in the course of the menstrual cycle of a woman is very often called the "Knaus method" or the "Ogino-Knaus method" or the "Ogino-Smulders method." Which is the correct description?

First of all we should like to stress again that the alternation of fertile and sterile days is a perfectly *natural* phenomenon. The expression "method" gives rise to misunderstandings and unjustifiable comparisons with artificial "contraceptive methods."

Today a savant of world renown, Dr. Hermann Knaus was professor of gynecology at Graz University when he devised the method for determining the time of ovulation. Shortly afterward he was appointed head of the gynecological clinic at the University of Prague, where he remained until the end of the Second World War. Although equally eminent as scientist and as clinician, Knaus did not find in his native Austria, after the war, that full measure of recognition which was due to him, and in this respect he has shared the fate of most pioneers. Knaus continues to devote himself, as doctor and scientist, to the good of mankind. For many years he has been director of the obstetrical and gynecological department in the hospital at Vienna-Lainz. Knaus is the outstanding expert today in the field of scientific investigation into the propagation of the human race. All important discoveries concerning the sterile days in women derive from him.

As we have shown, ovulation (the release of the ovum) takes place between the 12th and 16th day before the next menstruation. Professor Knaus teaches that in healthy women, provided that no upsetting factors intervene, ovulation always occurs on the 15th day before the coming menstruation. We have seen in an earlier section that the days from the 12th to the 19th before the start of the next menstruation must be regarded as fertile. According to Professor Knaus, as ovulation normally takes place in a healthy woman on the 15th day before the next menstruation, it is sufficient to practice abstinence from the 14th day to the 18th day, inclusive, before the next menstruation.

We are of the opinion—and in this we are in agreement with Professor Knaus—that the accurate calculation of the days of abstinence should be carried out under medical guidance. But since this work is intended for the general public, we have added several days to our basic calculation of this period of abstinence because reliance on the physiological law alone is not sufficient in order to avoid conception; allowance must be made for the variations which will most probably occur—the cycle variations of some few days about which we will speak further in Part Two. Other writers support this viewpoint. Besides Ogino and Smulders, there are Latz, Holt, Stecher, Palmer, and Ockel.

In his work, *Die fruchtbaren und unfruchtbaren Tage der Frau* (p. 58), Professor Knaus stresses the fact that from "a major change in the normal routine of life . . . changes in the feminine cycle" can be expected. These changes can lead to "an incalculable dislocation of the ovulation time."

Figure 14 shows the difference in determining the sterile days according to Knaus and Ogino.

Because of practical differences, one could place in opposition to the "Knaus method" the "Ogino method of calculation" or "Smulders method of adaptation." But to the last two designations should be added, "based on the findings of Knaus," since the decisive scientific pronouncements on the time of ovulation, the length of life of the ovum, and the viability of the spermatozoa come from him. We are following a custom long established in the world of science of honoring and perpetuating the name of the discoverer by calling his discovery after him. Thus we think of Watt, Volta, Ampère, Roentgen, and others. In this sense, it is only right and proper to speak of "the Knaus method."

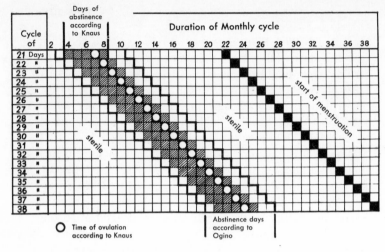

Fig. 14

In conclusion, we may draw a comparison—though they are always odious—to illustrate the respective merits of the experts who blazed the trail to the new method. Knaus invented the engine, so to speak, he devised and constructed it; Ogino knew how the tracks should be laid, and Smulders devised the time-table which, ensuring the best connections, is still in use today. None of the three was superfluous, we can dispense with no one of them, and they have all equally earned our thanks.

For those who read German, Dr. Knaus' two most important works on the subject of periodic sterility in women are: *Die Physiologie der Zeugung des Menschen*, 4th ed., Vienna, 1953, and *Die fruchtbaren und unfruchtbaren Tage, und deren richtige Berechnung*, 10th ed., Munich.

PART TWO

THE PRACTICE OF
NATURAL BIRTH CONTROL

III

THE PATTERNS OF THE CYCLE

1. From theory to practice

In Chapter II, §4, "The fertile and sterile days in women," we explained the general biological laws; we showed on what days of the menstrual cycle a woman is fertile, and on what days she is not. That section must be thoroughly understood if the method is to be put to practical use.

A knowledge of the natural laws limited to what is said about them in that chapter is *not at all sufficient*. To put the method into practice without taking into consideration the contents of the following chapters is to run the risk of bitter disappointment. One must know how these laws we have described *apply in individual cases*, how theory is to be adapted correctly to practice—in other words, the process, or method, must be understood. Hereunder we shall describe it in detail.

2. The cycles, their variations, and pattern

a) *The accurate calculation of the cycle days*

An indispensable prerequisite for an effective application of the method of periodic abstinence is an *accurate knowledge of the*

37

cycle pattern of the woman concerned. We shall see how this is determined.

We already know that a cycle consists of *the number of days which elapse from the first day of menstruation to the last day before the next menstruation.*

So the first day on which bleeding occurs is the first day of the cycle. The last day before the start of the next flow is the last day of the cycle. On that day the cycle finishes. The first day on which bleeding next occurs must not be included in the preceding cycle because it already forms part of the next cycle. Care must be exercised in order to avoid mistakes in the calculation of the days. Thus, if menstruation starts on the 29th day, the cycle has lasted 28 days—not 29! The 29th day does not form part of the preceding, but of the new, cycle. This will be clearly seen in Figure 15.

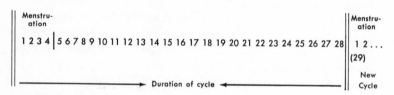

Fig. 15.   A 28-day cycle

b) *There is no standard cycle of 28 days*

It is necessary to issue a warning about a widespread error. Many believe that menstruation recurs regularly every 28 days, as a result of which this cycle is falsely described as the "normal cycle."

This notion is completely erroneous. In point of fact there is no normal cycle in a woman, nor in the long run does menstruation recur with absolute regularity. When in former times doctors spoke of a cycle of four weeks, they meant by this an average period of four weeks, with variations of a few days one way or the other. For the application of our method, a rough average of this kind is not sufficient; the exact length of the cycle must be calculated according to the days and not according to the weeks. Any woman who up to now has been under the impression that her period recurs exactly after the lapse of 28 days would do well to rid herself of such a belief; otherwise she is liable to be gravely disillusioned.

Every woman should keep an accurate and regular note of her cycles.

c) The cycles of every woman are different

Careful observations made in different countries have shown that each healthy woman has a very different cycle length. It was found that while many always had very short cycles—for example, of little more than three weeks—others again had very long cycles of about five weeks.

Among healthy Japanese women, Ogino found normal cycles of up to 45 days. European and American doctors ascertained that the cycles of healthy women vary between 22 and 36 days. Cycles in excess of 36 days were found in only 3 per cent, and cycles of less than 24 days in only 2 per cent of cases. The cycles of 95 per cent of the women lay between 24 and 36 days; of 78 per cent, between 25 and 31 days. Cycles of 21 days or less may be regarded as abnormal.

From a statistical survey by Dr. Latz of Chicago, it emerged that a large group of women collectively had individual cycles of the following relative frequency:

Duration of cycle:

22	23	24	25	26	27	28	29	30	31	32	33	34	35	36	37	days and over

Frequency:

0.5	3	6	11	13	15	16	12	8	6	4	2	1	1	1	0.5	per cent

The 28-day cycle, therefore, formed only one-sixth of all the cycles surveyed. Cycles shorter than 28 days appeared in 48 per cent, and those longer than 28 days in 35.5 per cent of cases. Of the women investigated by Latz, 96 per cent had cycles ranging between 23 and 33 days.

The preceding figures relate to a large group of women taken as a whole. They possess no value for the individual case.

A study of individual cases disclosed, according to Professor Latz, that 14 per cent of women always have cycles shorter than 28 days, while 6 per cent always have cycles longer than 28 days. Further, while it is true that 80 per cent of women have cycles of 28 days, nevertheless they have them together with cycles of other durations. On the average, only every fifth cycle is of 28 days' duration.

d) The length of the cycle varies from month to month— amount of variation

A second important fact, which was stated at the same time, is that, in the same woman, successive cycles are of different lengths. Sometimes, although rarely, it can happen that a woman has a cycle of uniform length for months—a cycle, for instance, of 29 days for four consecutive months, but so far no case has ever been found of a woman having a cycle of exactly uniform length twelve or more consecutive times: in all women the length of the cycle varies by a few days from month to month. One woman, for example, was found to have the following cycles: 27, 29, 27, 30, 28, 27, 29, 29, 30, 27, 28, 30 days. In that year her shortest cycle was 27 days and her longest, 30 days. Her cycles, therefore, fluctuated between 27 and 30 days.

The extent of the variation with this woman amounts to 4 days (27, 28, 29, and 30). This extent of variation is known as the cycle pattern of the woman concerned, and this woman, accordingly, would be said to have a cycle pattern of 27 to 30 days. Every woman has her own cycle pattern.

e) The cycle pattern

The only way in which a woman can establish her cycle pattern is to observe and record accurately the length of each successive cycle over a period of at least a year. The best method of doing this is to mark unfailingly on a calendar the first day of menstruation (flow of blood). At the onset of the next menstruation, the number of days the previous cycle has lasted should be accurately counted and this recorded in the calendar. When consecutive cycles have been observed over a period of a year and their lengths duly recorded, one may learn from this the cycle pattern. For example, cycle lengths of 27, 25, 27, 26, 28, 25, 27, 26, 25, 27, 28, 26, the shortest cycle being 25 and the longest 28, disclose a cycle pattern of 25 to 28 days.

During the course of an accurate observation of cycles one finds that, here and there, even among healthy women, an unexpected deviation from the habitual cycle pattern may arise, that now and then a cycle does not, so to speak, fit into the general picture. Different circumstances—as we shall explain later in greater detail—have their influence on the length of the cycle and can bring about an upset in its normal course. These isolated disturbances need not be taken into consideration in determining the cycle pattern of the woman concerned, but they must be taken into account in the interests of the safety of the method, as we shall see further on.

Consider this example: A woman observed the following cycles: 25, 24, 26, 24, 32, 28, 26, 27, 24, 26, 28, 27. The shortest cycle is 24 days, the longest, 28 days. The cycle pattern is 24 to 28 days. The one deviation (32 days) is not considered.

f) The most frequent cycle pattern among healthy women

As we have mentioned, there is no normal cycle applicable to all women; every woman has her own individual cycle pattern which is in conformity with her general condition.

A woman, for example, who has a cycle pattern of 28 to 30 days, knows that when a cycle starts it will last 28, 29, or 30 days (unless an accidental upset occurs).

The cycle pattern of 28 to 30 days can have a cycle of three different lengths—28, 29, or 30 days. Such a cycle pattern is said to be triple.

Only 5 per cent to 6 per cent of women have a triple cycle pattern.

Double cycle patterns—for example, of a constant 30 or 31 days—either never occur at all or else are extremely rare. According to Dr. Latz they occur in 0.5 per cent of women.

The single cycle pattern of, for example, a uniform 29 days, does not exist.

Among healthy women, the quintuple cycle pattern is the one most frequently found, occurring in 26 per cent of cases.

A woman with a cycle pattern of 24 to 28 days obviously has a quintuple pattern, as her cycle can have five different lengths —24, 25, 26, 27, or 28 days.

The quadruple cycle pattern is also rather frequent; according to Latz it is found in 12 per cent of cases. A cycle pattern of 31 to 34 days, for example, is quadruple—31, 32, 33, 34.

The sextuple (22.5 per cent) and the septuple (17 per cent) cycle patterns are also very frequent, and must be regarded as quite normal.

The octuple cycle pattern Latz found in 11 per cent, the nonuple in 4 per cent, and the decuple in 1 per cent of the cases observed. One half of one per cent (0.5 per cent) of women had a margin of variation of 11 days or more.

Dr. Latz of Chicago arrived at these results in 1942 after a study of 3,762 women, spread over months. Figure 16 summarizes the results of his investigation.

The quintuple cycle pattern, the most frequently occurring, is distinguished by a heavy outline in the diagram. Cases of less than 0.5 per cent are indicated by a small, unnumbered circle. All the figures given are naturally approximate only. Other investigators have arrived at substantially the same findings.

The commonest cycle pattern was that of 26 to 30 days which was found in 4.7 per cent of the women. Next in order came the cycle pattern of 25 to 29 days which was found in 4.4 per cent of cases.

	22	23	24	25	26	27	28	29	30	31	32	33	34	35	36	37	38	39		Summary
21		0	0	½	1	1	1	0	0											3½%
22			0	½	1	1	1½	½	0	0										4½%
23				½	1	3	3	2	1	½	0	0								11½%
24					1	2	4	3½	2½	1	½	0	0	0						15%
25					0	1	2½	4½	4	2½	1½	1	½	0	0					18%
26						0	1	2½	4½	3½	2	1½	1	½	0					17%
27							½	1	2	3	2½	2	2	1	0	0				14%
28								0	½	1	2	2	1½	2	0	0	0			9%
29									0	0	½	1	1	1	0	0	0			4%
30										0	0	0	½	½	0	0	0			1%
31												0	½	½	0	0				1%
32													0	0	0					0%
33													0	0						0%
34																				0%
35																				
																				99½%

Fig. 16. Note: The O's in the chart have been used to indicate a percentage of less than ½%. Although the actual percentages are not given, they have been included in the totals under the Summary column.

3. Difficulties, disturbances, and variations

a) Difficulties in determining the cycle pattern

Many women claim to have had a 14-day cycle, a statement which is not to be accepted. There are women, as a matter of fact, who have bleeding from the sexual organs roughly every two weeks, but this does not mean that a true menstruation always occurs. With such women the bleeding usually alternates —the first time it is strong and lasts about four days or more (as in normal menstruation), the next time (about 14 days later) it is weak and lasts one or two days only. These women usually have a cycle pattern of roughly 4 *weeks*. In the middle of the cycle, at the time of ovulation, they have another bleeding which they confuse with menstruation but which is *ovular bleeding* (also called "false menstruation"). They must obviously reckon the length of their cycles from one true menstruation to the next true one, ignoring the intervening ovular bleeding.

For the inexperienced, it is sometimes difficult to decide whether the menstruation is true or not. Such women ought to consult a doctor who will make it clear to them which bleeding indicates the true menstruation. The taking of the temperature will also help to clear up the point (Chapter II, §2 b).

It can happen that one or two days before menstruation a light-brown to dark-brown colored fluid may be discharged. This discharge does not enter into the calculation of the days in a cycle. The cycle begins on that day on which the start of true menstruation is clearly observed.

b) Variable cycles

When a variation occurs in the cycle pattern under observation, it is sometimes difficult to say whether it is an exceptional variation which—as we have already stated—need not be taken into account when determining the cycle pattern, or whether the margin of variation in the cycle pattern is greater than had been hitherto observed, especially if the variation amounts to one or two days only. Let us suppose, for example, that throughout a period of at least a year only cycles of from 27 to 29 days were observed. Suddenly a cycle of 26 days occurs and a few months later, following a mountain trip, a cycle of 36 days. The cycle of 26 days will certainly be counted as part of the normal margin of variation, because *with triple cycle patterns one must always be cautious* and allow for the possibility that the observation time up to this, even though it has extended beyond a year, may still have been too short to enable a correct cycle pattern to be determined. Hence, in the example under consideration, one would regard the cycle pattern from now on to be one of 26 to 29 days. Similar caution should be exercised in respect to quadruple cycle patterns. No cycle pattern should be taken to be defined if the margin of variation is less than five.

The other deviation in the above example, the single cycle of 36 days, does not affect the calculation of the cycle pattern. It extends too far beyond the customary length of the cycles, and, moreover, one knows on this occasion why there occurred so much longer a cycle—that strenuous mountain climbing which retarded ovulation.

An abnormal deviation must not be included in the calculation of the cycle pattern when one is in a position to supply a reason for the alteration—for example, a feverish illness, excessive exertion, an automobile accident, etc.

When no discernible reason can be found to explain the alteration in the length of the cycle, and when the variation is not considerable—one or two days only—the new cycle then probably forms part of the cycle pattern and should be included in it. Observation should be continued to see whether the new cycle recurs.

Another point that must be taken into consideration is that the new cycle very probably forms part of the cycle pattern if its length variation lies in the direction of the 28-day cycle. For example: A woman has hitherto had a cycle pattern of 31 to 34 days. Then, for the first time, a cycle of 30 days occurs. This will be counted as part of the normal variation margin and from thenceforward she will consider her cycle pattern to be one of 30 to 34 days.

In every case the course of the cycles must be *continually observed*. Sometimes it may take several years before a woman can see her cycle pattern in full clarity.

Ogino cites a case from his own practice—unfortunately without giving precise data—where a woman, as the result of three years' observation, was held to have a triple cycle pattern. Nevertheless, at the expiration of a further three years, it was established that she had an octuple cycle pattern!

c) *Disturbances in the course of the cycle*

The woman who wishes to avoid conception through the practice of periodic abstinence should have an exact knowledge of her own peculiar cycle and of its normal pattern, as well as of the causes of the upsets to which she is subject.

As we have stressed many times, outside circumstances can exert a disturbing influence upon the course of the cycle. The effect differs in accordance with the type of disturbance and the time at which it occurs. When the disturbance occurs during the first few days of the cycle, it can cause ovulation to be either precipitated or retarded. Whether premature ovulation is likely is debatable and hardly probable. On the other hand, retarded ovulation, due to disturbing influences, has been observed many times.

Delay in ovulation usually brings about an alteration in the fertile days. Special attention should, therefore, be paid to these disturbances.

When the disturbing influence occurs toward the middle of the cycle, that is to say at the time of ovulation, it may result in the abrupt interruption of the cycle. A bleeding may occur, which lasts from two to three days and resembles true menstruation, although this is not the case. Then a new cycle starts just as if menstruation had occurred.

During the ovulation period, the disturbing factor may have yet another effect—it may not be noticed that the new cycle has been interrupted; no discharge takes place, no yellow body is formed, but a new follicle develops. Unnoticed, a new cycle begins, and after the follicular phase peculiar to the woman in question, there is a second ovulatory episode and, two weeks later, normal menstruation takes place. Consequently, there were two ovulatory episodes, instead of one, between two widely separated menstruations. In such a case one speaks, somewhat inaccurately, of a double cycle.

When the disturbance occurs *after* ovulation has taken place and the ovum is perhaps already dead, then in this case menstruation may begin immediately. On the other hand, the opposite can happen and menstruation may be delayed beyond its expected date.

Some illnesses of an organic or functional nature have the effect of making the course of the cycles completely irregular, i.e., 29, 14, 36, 28, 45, 16 . . . days.

d) Variations in the cycle pattern

Healthy women can also have cycles of varied pattern. This variation may be brought about by different living conditions, by change of climate or of diet, by slimming, by the taking of certain medicines, especially hormone preparations, after a serious illness, etc. Marriage can likewise exercise a certain influence, as equally can the changing over from contraceptives to natural sex relations, etc., etc. It is therefore essential to *check continually the length of the cycle.*

One must be especially careful if, up to the present, a *variation margin of less than 5 days* has been found—for example, a **triple** cycle pattern only.

4. The undulatory movement of the cycle pattern

The Swiss gynecologist, Dr. Stecher, points out in his book *Zeitwahl in der Ehe* (Continence in Marriage) that all cycle patterns have the tendency to move in the direction of the median one of 28 days. His attention was drawn to this "undulatory movement" of the cycle pattern by the works of the Dutch gynecologist, Dr. Holt.

Existing technical literature does not give any explanation for this remarkable phenomenon. It appears to us that behind it is hidden a great natural law connected with the natural regulation of the sex of progeny. (We shall return to this in Chapter VI, §5 d.)

To illustrate the practical conclusions to be drawn from the undulatory movement of the cycles: A woman who, as a result of observations extending over a year, has fixed her cycle pattern as one of 23 to 27 days should expect a cycle of 28 days to appear shortly. Another who perhaps has so far observed a cycle pattern of 33 to 36 days, should expect a cycle of 32 or 31 days to occur in the near future.

It is especially important to pay attention to the undulatory movement if a triple cycle pattern only has hitherto been observed.

To explain how the undulatory movement works, we show in Fig. 17 (from *Zeitwahl in der Ehe*) the cycle pattern of a woman which was observed by Dr. Stecher for over 17 years.

The chart confirms what Professor Knaus had already found, namely, that as one grows older there is a tendency for the cycle pattern to become shorter.

Compare the evolution of the cyclic patterns with the examples given in Chapter IX.

5. The influence of age on the cycle

Of the influence of age on the cycle pattern at the various stages of a woman's life the following can be said:

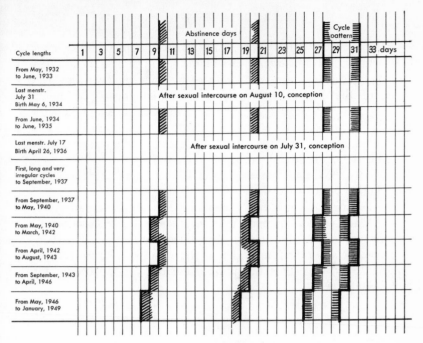

Fig. 17

Young girls, even when perfectly healthy, are apt to have very irregular cycles for a year or two after the first menstruation. Not having reached full sexual maturity, the young girl has not yet found her personal cycle pattern.

Among fully developed, healthy women there prevails a greater stability in the cycle pattern. The undulatory movement is generally slow.

The cycles are nearly always disturbed after a birth; menstruation usually fails to appear for a few months (generally only two or three, but in some women for a half year or longer). Much depends on whether or not she is nursing her child. Then follow, as a rule, very irregular cycles. Often they are very long— around 50 to 60 days. It can happen, however, that even the first cycles after a birth are short. The cessation of breast feeding generally causes a fresh disturbance. A few months later menstruation mostly resumes its normal flow, but a change in the cycle pattern is sometimes observed after childbirth. A woman, who for several years before the birth of her child had had a cycle pattern of 26 to 29 days, may discover after the birth that her cycle pattern is gradually lengthening to one of 28 to 32 days, or that the pattern is shortening to about 24 to 27 days. The new cycle pattern then usually remains until the next pregnancy. On the other hand, the cycle pattern often remains unchanged after childbirth.

As we said in an earlier paragraph, the cycle pattern tends to shorten with the passing of the years.

During the climacteric, the cycles generally are very irregular.

Many women maintain that the change in the seasons exercises a definite influence on their cycle pattern, and that every year the same variations occur at the same periods, but the evidence available does not provide grounds for supporting this contention.

IV

SELF-KNOWLEDGE IS ESSENTIAL

1. Every woman is different

Dr. Smulders tirelessly stresses that the determination of the fertile and sterile days is an individual matter for every woman and ideally should be left in the hands of an experienced doctor. A general rule of calculation is not enough; personal idiosyncrasies, that is, individuality, must be taken into account.

Though all have the same human nature created by God, it is known that no two human beings are completely alike in every respect. Each one is marked by definite characteristics upon which heredity, environment, climate, diet, education, mode of life, and living habits have all a certain influence.

The individual differences of each person show themselves in many ways—in the shape of the body, the height, the color of the skin, the hair and eyes, and especially in the lineaments of the face, in the lines of the hand, the fingerprints, and even the composition of the blood. They are further displayed in the temperament and character, the measure of resistance to surrounding influences and to illness, the response to excitement. They show in personal deportment, for example, in the walk, the bearing, the tone of the voice, and the handwriting.

The personal characteristics of the woman are expressed in yet another way—through the shape of her cycle patterns.

51

a) By the *duration*. There are certain types of women who always have relatively short cycles of, for example, 24 to 27 days; others, with different personal characteristics, always have long cycles of, let us say, 31 to 34 days. Between these two extremes, every shade of gradation exists, as we have seen in a previous section.

b) By the *degree of variation* in the different cycle patterns. There is a wide difference to be found among different women, but, in most cases, as we already know, it varies from 3 to 7 days.

c) By the *undulating movement* of the cycle pattern. Unfortunately, insufficient information has been gathered on this subject.

d) By the *period in life* when the first menstruation occurs and the period when the climacteric begins.

e) By the *sensitivity of the cycle to disturbances*. In some women outside influences of a disturbing nature can easily alter the habitual rhythm of their periodic course; on the other hand, others can withstand grave shocks without any attendant upset in their cycles. In this, too, all gradations are found between these two extremes.

All these differences in cycle behavior correspond to definite *differences in a woman's nature*. They are displayed, among other ways, in a marked preference for a certain type of man. Not every man appeals to every woman. A woman's type, which expresses itself in her cycle peculiarities, is a determining factor in the choice of partner and hence in the bringing about of specific marriages. In this way nature exercises a regulating influence on the procreation of specific progeny. Unfortunately we are very ill-informed upon this matter, but great mysteries of nature lie hidden here.

The sexual peculiarities of a woman, which are reflected in her individual cycle pattern, result from the co-operation and opposition of various stimuli and various inhibitions which stem from several sources. The most important of these are the endocrine glands, especially the pituitary, which transmit their hormones to the blood, the ovaries, and perhaps also the dien-cephalon. Metabolism, the nervous system, and psychical experiences also exert an effect.

2. Influences which a woman must study

A woman wishing to avoid conception by periodic abstinence must not only know the exact pattern of her cycles but also her *sensitivity to disturbances*. She must know whether, and in what way, she reacts to specific events or experiences through any alteration in the course of her cycle.

Disturbing influences may be produced by:

a) *Circumstances*—for example, a change of climate, a different altitude (e.g., mountain climbing), journeys, especially journeys involving differences in time keeping (e.g., a trip from Europe to America or vice versa), for with such a change of place the daily temperature curve must first be adjusted; again, any change in the usual mode of life, such as exceptionally hard work, too much effort, undue activity in sports, etc. We must also mention any unusual change of food, special diets, thermal treatment, slimming courses, etc.

b) *Organic troubles*, infections accompanied by high fever, accidents or severe injuries, any illness which necessitates special medical treatment, whether by way of surgical operation or injections, especially of hormones, or of sulfanilamides or antibiotics, such as penicillin; or treatment with preparations containing an iodine or mercury or arsenic base, and others.

c) They may also be produced by *intense emotional experiences* such as an unwonted great joy or shock—an accident, deep grief caused by a death, a terrifying experience, etc.

d) Finally they may be caused by changes in the *sexual behavior*, in the marriage itself, prolonged interruption of sexual union, the transition from contraceptive to natural sexual relations. We shall deal in a later section with the disturbances in the cyclic pattern which arise after childbirth or miscarriage, and during breast feeding and weaning.

Obviously no woman could possibly remember all these things, and so it is essential to make an accurate note of them.

3. The keeping of a menstrual calendar

Young girls should be trained to keep a menstrual calendar from the onset of the first menstruation to its last appearance in the climacteric years.

For this purpose, we have added to the book a Chart Sheet with the necessary explanations. This has also the advantage of making possible the recording of the temperature on waking (see §4 below) in a simple and clear form. The Chart Sheet— or any good menstrual calendar—provides a sound basis for the determination of the fertile and sterile days. On this Chart Sheet should be recorded, with precise dates, everything relating to the course of the cycle—the start of menstruation and its duration, symptoms of ovulation (for example, intermenstrual pain), pregnancies, births, period of breast feeding, and all experiences which, as we have mentioned in the preceding section, can produce a disturbance of the normal course of the cycle.

A woman who has been keeping such a calendar for a long time learns from experience whether and to what extent her reaction to a certain occurrence is reflected in an alteration of her cycle. She will thus guard herself against mistakes when using periodic abstinence to avoid conception.

Every woman should keep a carefully annotated Chart Sheet (or menstruation calendar and temperature chart) and show it to her doctor when she is ill.

4. Recording of temperature curves

In addition to keeping a menstrual calendar, every woman must continuously and accurately record her temperature curve, as we have said in Chapter II, §2 b. When she has become more experienced, she can reduce the temperature readings to a few specific days, those days shortly before the next expected date of ovulation. The best system is to begin the temperature readings on the 18th day before the earliest expected onset of the next menstruation, that is to say, calculating back from the *shortest* cycle in her cycle pattern. The temperature readings must continue until she is certain from the temperature curve that ovulation has taken place. (See Chapter VI, §4 c.)

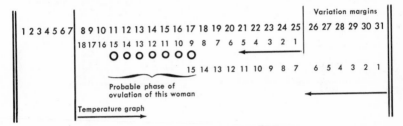

Fig. 18.   Cycle pattern of 25 to 31 days

An example may help to explain (see Fig. 18). Let us suppose that a woman has a cycle pattern of 25 to 31 days. Calculating back from the shortest cycle (the one of 25 days), ovulation, which we know takes place on the 15th day before the next menstruation (see Chapter II, §1 b), will occur on the 11th day of the cycle. Now, as a measure of caution, she must start temperature readings as early as the 8th day of the cycle, which would be on the 18th day before the earliest expected menstruation would begin.

If one does not want to plot the temperature readings in graph form, it is just as effective to use the Chart Sheet at the back of this book, or any other suitable memorandum sheet or notebook. Figure 19 is an example of such a record as given by another writer.

A continual and accurate recording of the temperature curve during the first months of pregnancy is of the utmost importance for all women, but especially for those who tend to have

Name:

Month — March						Month — April					
date	temp.	notes	date	temp.	notes	date	temp.	notes	date	temp.	notes
1			16	98.6		1		m	16	98.7	
2		m	17	98.9		2		m	17	98.9	
3		m	18	98.7		3		m	18	98.7	
4		m	19	98.7		4	97.3		19	98.7	
5		m	20	98.6		5	97.9		20	98.6	
6		m	21	98.9		6	97.7		21	98.7	
7	97.5		22	98.6		7	97.7		22	98.9	
8	97.7		23	98.7		8	97.5		23	98.7	
9	97.5		24	98.7		9	98		24	98.6	
10	97.8		25	98.6		10	97.7		25	98.9	
11	97.7		26	98.9		11	97.8		26	98.	
12	97.7		27	98.7		12	98.9		27		m
13	97.5		28	98.7		13	98.7		28		m
14	97.8		29	98.2		14	98.9		29		m
15	97.5		30		m	15	98.6		30		m
			31		m						

Fig. 19

miscarriages. A fall in temperature indicates a weakening of the action of the yellow body and a consequent danger of miscarriage. The advice of a doctor should be sought without delay.

5. The glucose test

In recent years the glucose test for determining the time of ovulation has assumed very considerable importance.

As we have said in Chapter II, §2 c, the uterine mucus (more correctly, the cervical mucus), contains a certain quantity of glucose during the days of ovulation; during the other days of the cycle, on the other hand, glucose is not present in the mucus of healthy women. On the day of ovulation, the glucose content in the mucus is particularly high. Its presence can be detected quite easily by means of the test paper already mentioned or by other reactive tests. Some women carry out the tests themselves, and they maintain that the procedure is simple and easy to learn, needing no special knowledge or preliminary instruction. We, however, believe that it is more advisable that every woman, at least in the beginning, should seek assistance from either a doctor or a nurse.

When doctors in the United States carried out their first tests of this new method, they inserted the chemically treated test paper (or a pad impregnated with reagent substances) directly into the female genital organs (cervical canal). They left the testing material in place for a few minutes to see if it became colored. Certain objections were raised against this method as it was feared that the chemically treated test substances could cause cancer.

Then G. & M. Laboratories, Inc., of Henderson, Kentucky, developed an improved process. They put on the market a simple tampon, about 6 inches in length and made from plastic material, called a "Rhythm Meter." This is not injurious to health and is easily kept clean. In the top, removable end of the tampon the transfer paper, supplied by the firm, is fixed. The paper contains no chemical substance whatever; it is ordinary plain paper, with specific absorbency and tension.

Complete with this harmless paper, the tampon is inserted into the vagina in such a way as to press lightly on the neck of the uterus (cervix). (Exact instructions and diagrams are given on the package.) The tampon is left in position for about a half minute so that the transfer paper can become completely soaked with mucus. The tampon is then removed, the wet transfer paper is pressed gently against the prepared test paper and is left in contact with it for some minutes to see if coloration takes place. The only difficulty in the process lies in learning how to bring the tampon to the correct position so that the paper may soak up the cervical mucus.

The test paper is not supplied with the tampon but must be purchased separately from a druggist. There are various test substances, and the suppliers give precise directions with every package. Tes-Tape, manufactured by the firm of Eli Lilly & Co., Indianapolis, Indiana, is much used. On the day of ovulation this paper turns a very deep, dark green. Clinistix, of the Ames

Company, is also popular. The effect of the sugar content on the day of ovulation is to turn this a deep blue.

To determine the fertile and sterile days it is essential that *initially the glucose test be made every day*, except during the menstruation period. The coloration must be entered on the Chart Sheet every day. It is best to use single letters: *n* for nil; *lg* for light green; *dg* for dark green. With Clinistix it would be: *bb*—bright blue; *db*—dark blue.

The day on which the Tes-Tape becomes dark green (dark blue in the case of Clinistix) is the day of ovulation. At the end of the cycle, at the onset of the next menstruation, one can verify whether the ovulation day, established with the aid of the glucose test, has in fact taken place around the 15th day before the succeeding menstruation. The check must be made for several months before one can be sure that the glucose test is being made correctly and accurate results being obtained. The glucose test can be relied upon with confidence only when the memoranda made over a period of many months confirm that the time of ovulation, as determined by the glucose test, always lies about 15 days before the start of the next menstruation.

In later months the check can be relaxed, for by then one will know from experience the earliest time at which ovulation takes place. The glucose test should then begin *4 days* before the earliest expected onset of ovulation and should be continued for *3 days* after the appearance of the dark-green color (or the dark blue). In this way the glucose test need only be made for about a week in the course of each cycle; this is sufficient for healthy women who have already acquired experience of the system.

If the glucose test shows that the ovulation day indicated by the color always deviates considerably from the calculated ovulation time (namely, the 15th day before the next menstruation); or if several color changes occur in the one cycle; or, again, if the coloration has shown on several or all days during the cycle; then a doctor should be consulted. The presence of glucose could be caused by disease.

In healthy women it can also happen that occasionally *no ovulation* can be detected during the whole cycle, but, if this is a rare occurrence, there is no cause for worry. In young, growing girls there is often no ovulation, as likewise in the climacteric years, during the breast-feeding period, and sometimes for no apparent reason.

We already know that in every cycle there is a *double* set of sterile days; the first occurs after menstruation up to the 4th day before the presumed earliest date to be expected for ovulation; the second consists of the last 11 days of the cycle. Neither by means of the glucose test nor by temperature reading can the sterile days between menstruation and the next ovulation be determined with certainty. *They must be calculated every time.* Nevertheless, once the ovulation day has been determined, either by the glucose test or by the temperature chart, it is known that from the *4th day* after ovulation up to the next menstruation there is no fear of pregnancy. (See Fig. 20.)

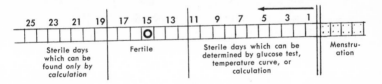

Fig. 20

V

"CYCLE SCIENCE"

1. How it began

Fortunately the disturbances which are liable to result in undesired pregnancies are not very frequent. It must be confessed,
however, that we still do not know much about the course of
the cycle and the influences to which it is subjected. A vast
field of investigation here awaits the specialists.

Much has become clearer in recent years, for, since the discoveries of Knaus and Ogino, increased attention has been paid
to the peculiarities of the cyclic courses and there has developed
what one might call a special "cycle science." Its beginnings go
back to Dr. Smulders, the distinguished Dutch physician, who,
unfortunately, died in 1939. His compatriot, Dr. Holt, a gynecologist, carried on the work, and was later followed by Professor Latz, Professor Miller, and other Americans. Deserving
of special mention are the labors of Dr. Stecher, a Swiss specialist.

2. Its problems

First and foremost the task is to go deeply into and to solve
fully those problems which we have already mentioned. An
explanation will have to be found as to why individual cycles

are different and why cycle patterns have such diverse variations, and how it comes about that the period between the
start of menstruation and the ovulation which follows it, the
follicular phase, displays such great differences in duration.

To be considered and explained is the reason why some
women have 15 menstruations annually, while others have only
9, although both are in equally good health; why most women
have 13 menstruations a year; why, in healthy women, the
follicular phase lasts sometimes for 8 days and sometimes for
21 days. In both cases, nature achieves the same object; namely,
to provide an ovum capable of being fertilized. (See Fig. 21.)

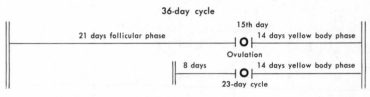

36-day cycle

21 days follicular phase

15th day

14 days yellow body phase

Ovulation

8 days

14 days yellow body phase

23-day cycle

Fig. 21

Also unexplained is the connection between these cycle
differences and hereditary traits, peculiarities of character and
temperament, the regularity of the cycle, and sensitivity to disturbances. Finally, in what way are they related to the choice
of partner, to the sex and the hereditary dispositions of the
nascent child?

All this would lead up to the questions of whether it would be
possible deliberately to influence the cycle pattern without in-
juriously affecting the health of the woman.

3. Erroneous conclusions from statistics

The fundamental and most important discovery to emerge from
the scientific study of the cycle is the fact that every woman
has to be studied personally and *individually* for the determination of her fertile and sterile days. The observation of numbers

of women and the compilation of experiences gathered can indeed lead to interesting statistics, but we must never forget that such general or frequency statistics are worthless for individual application.

Unfortunately this has not always been recognized. Thus, for example, Dr. A. Niedermeyer, in his book *Fakultative Sterilität* (Capellmann-Niedermeyer, 1931), utilized the frequency curves drawn up by Siegel, Bolaffio, and others during the First World War to prove that the Knaus theory was inaccurate. Figure 22 shows how Siegel's frequency curve appeared.

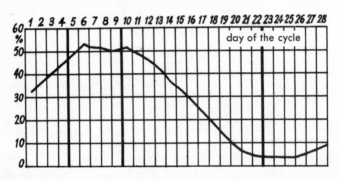

Fig. 22. Conception curve according to Siegel (percentages based on observation of 300 cases)

It is precisely because the Knaus method is accurate that the frequency curves must appear roughly like those found by Siegel and others, for all are more or less similar.

If we arrange together in a comprehensive graph the observations of different cycle lengths in relation to their frequency made by Latz, and record therein the fertile days to each individual cycle pattern, we shall get the picture shown in Fig. 23. From this graph we can deduce how many women are fertile on the different days of the cycle, counting from the start of menstruation. This can be seen from the perpendicular distance between the upper and lower lines of the curve of the particular day of the cycle.

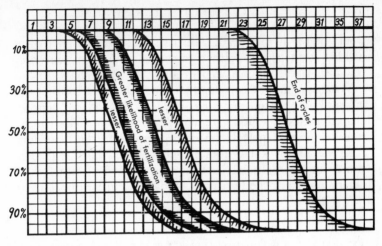

Fig. 23

These distances produce a new graph (Fig. 24) which is similar to that found by the earlier writers, Siegel and others. The explanation for their diversity is to be found in the inaccuracy of earlier investigations, a fact which was pointed out by Holt in 1931.

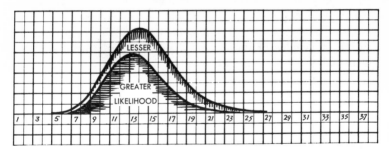

Fig. 24

To draw the conclusion from such frequency statistics—as unfortunately is still occasionally done—that for every woman the possibility of conception begins on the fourth day of her cycle, then increases for a certain time, finally lessens but continues until the end of the cycle, is as much a mistake as it would be to say that death statistics show that every one of us will live to the age of 67, then 30 per cent will die of cancer, 30 per cent of heart disease, 20 per cent of apoplexy, etc.

What is a law of frequency statistics is not a law for the individual. From a frequency curve, in which the different personal characteristics of a group are united to form one collective picture, one cannot postulate a law applicable to the individual.

As we already know from Chapter II, §4, the rule demonstrated in Fig. 25 holds good in every individual case for the determination of the fertile and sterile days in healthy women.

Fig. 25

4. Its difficulties

In January, 1952, through a study on the rhythm of the menstrual cycle published in the *Deutschen Medizinischen Wochenschrift* (No. 15), Professor Knaus made a valuable contribution to the knowledge of the cycle. Disagreeing with the old, false idea that the glands of the pituitary body directed the cyclic process, Knaus showed that the rhythm of the menstrual cycle is directed by the ovaries.

How the mysteries hidden behind these cycle peculiarities are a part of the ultimate problems of life is expressed by the learned author in these impressive words with which he concludes his article:

Thus the question of the localization of the cause of the rhythm would appear to be answered, but the problem of the *origin of the motive power which determines the periodicity of the cycle* is not solved. This vital process, which lies outside the range of our understanding, is hidden in the cells of the germinal epithelium of the ovaries, the only tissue of the female body which could possibly supply the material, endowed with such astonishing powers, necessary for the conservation of the species which is its issue. Just as we are unable to imagine how this wonderful multiplicity of energy, closely linked in form and function, is rooted in the chromosomes of the fertilized ovum, we are also unable to follow the mysterious activity of the cells in which can be seen the beginning of the mystery of life.

VI

GUIDANCE FOR HEALTHY
WOMEN

1. The calculation of the fertile and sterile days

The sterile days can be calculated only when the woman in question has an accurate knowledge of her cycle pattern. To arrive at this, the cycles must have been noted in a menstrual calendar for a period of not less than one year.

In Chapter II we reached the conclusion that the *fertile* days in a woman are those from the 12th to the 19th day before the forthcoming menstruation. The days before and after these days are *sterile*. Sterile are: the last 11 days before the onset of the forthcoming menstruation; the days further removed than the 19th day before the onset of the next menstruation, that is, the 20th, 21st, 22nd, 23rd, etc. day before the next menstruation.

If a woman has a cycle of 30 days, for example, we get the picture as shown in Fig. 26. The fertile days are from the 12th to the 19th day before the next menstruation. The sterile days in this cycle are the last 11 days and the period between the 20th and 30th day before the next menstruation.

To calculate a woman's fertile and sterile days one must, therefore, count back from the expected date of the next menstruation. The most important factor in the computation of the "dangerous" days is to know when the next menstruation will commence, but that is something which can never be known accurately in advance because no woman has always cycles of equal length. It is sufficient, however, to know the earliest and latest date for the next menstruation and this can be determined by every healthy woman who knows her cycle pattern.

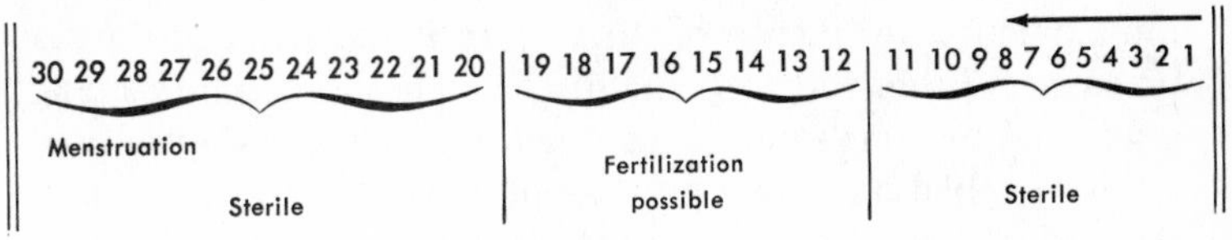

30 29 28 27 26 25 24 23 22 21 20	19 18 17 16 15 14 13 12	11 10 9 8 7 6 5 4 3 2 1
Menstruation	Fertilization	
Sterile	possible	Sterile

Fig. 26

It is only necessary to apply the calculation of the already known cycle pattern to each individual cycle in order to determine the fertile and sterile days of the entire cycle pattern.

For example, in the case of a cycle pattern of 27–30 days, it is known that the next menstruation can commence on the 27th, 28th, 29th, or 30th day after the onset of the last menstruation. We know that the fertile days are those from the 12th to the 19th day before the start of the new menstruation. It follows from this that the abstinence days are:

for the cycle of 27 days: 9th to 16th day of the cycle
for the cycle of 28 days: 10th to 17th day of the cycle
for the cycle of 29 days: 11th to 18th day of the cycle
for the cycle of 30 days: 12th to 19th day of the cycle

for the cycle pattern of 27–30 days: 9th to 19th day of the cycle

As the woman cannot tell whether this particular cycle will have a duration of 27, 28, 29, or 30 days, she must observe the abstinence days of all her possible cycles.

The same result is arrived at if simply the shortest and the longest cycles are considered, for the intermediary cycles are already included.

The abstinence days are:

for the cycle of 27 days:	9th to 16th day of the cycle
for the cycle of 30 days:	12th to 19th day of the cycle

for the cycle pattern of 27–30 days: 9th to 19th day of the cycle

A woman with a cycle pattern of 27–30 days is, consequently, sterile during the first 8 days of the cycle. From the 9th to the 19th day of the cycle there is a possibility of conception, so she must practice abstinence on these days if she wishes to avoid pregnancy. From the 20th day of the cycle she becomes sterile again, and remains so until the onset of the next menstruation.

The calculation, therefore, is not difficult. The important thing is to take into account the abstinence days which correspond to the longest cycle, and those which correspond to the shortest. Abstinence must be practiced on all these days.

If the calculation is made on a calendar, the dates of the fertile and sterile days are at once available. Take, for example, a woman who has a cycle pattern of 27–30 days. To determine her sterile days, she will first calculate, with the help of the calendar, the day on which the next menstruation should occur, basing her count this time on the shortest duration of her cycle. Having found this date, she will then add on the corresponding abstinence days, that is, the period from the 12th to the 19th day preceding this date, and she will mark these days on her calendar.

But her cycle this time could also occur in its longest form. Again with the aid of her calendar, she will calculate the expected date of her next menstruation, allowing this time for the longest duration period of her cycle. She will count back from this date and mark the fertile days in her calendar, that is, the period from the 12th to the 19th preceding this date. In short, the woman will calculate the fertile days corresponding to her shortest cycle and the fertile days corresponding to her longest cycle and regard all these days as abstinence days. The start of the fertile days is calculated from the shortest cycle; the end of the fertile days, from the longest cycle.

To give another example: a woman has observed the following cycles: 30, 29, 29, 36, 31, 29, 30, 31, 29, 29, 30, 30. The last menstruation occurred on July 4. She wants to find out on what days she should practice abstinence during this cycle and which days are the sterile ones. Her cycle pattern is 29–31 days (with one variation of 36 days). If this present cycle should be her shortest one of 29 days, then her next menstruation would begin on August 2. Counting 19 days back in the calendar from this date, the abstinence period is found to start on July 14.

If, on the contrary, her cycle should this time have its longest duration (31 days), the next menstruation will take place on the 32nd day, that is on August 4. The last 11 days of this, the longest cycle, are sterile, that is, from July 24 onward.

The "dangerous" days of the cycle pattern of 29–31 days are, therefore, from July 14 to July 23 (see Fig. 27).

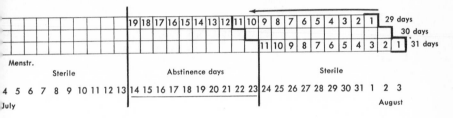

Fig. 27. Start of abstinence days: the shortest cycle less 19; end of abstinence days: the longest cycle less 11

Short résumé

1. Determination of the cycle pattern: How many days elapse between the first day of menstruation and the last day preceding the next menstruation? What are the longest and shortest cycles of the last 12 months? (Example: cycle pattern of 30–34 days.)

2. The start of the abstinence days is found by subtracting 19 days from the shortest cycle. (Example: 30 − 19 = 11.) The first 11 days in this example are sterile. The first day following, thus the 12th day of the cycle, marks the start of the abstinence period.

3. The end of the fertile days is calculated by deducting 11 days from the longest cycle. (Example: 34 − 11 = 23.) The abstinence period continues until the 23rd day of the cycle. For this cycle pattern the sterile days are the first 11 days and those extending from the 24th day of the cycle to the onset of the next menstruation.

The entire calculation, therefore, is quite simple.

Another example: cycle pattern of 25–28 days. Start of the last menstruation, September 12. Calculation: 25 − 19 = 6. Therefore, the first 6 days, September 12, 13, 14, 15, 16, and 17 are sterile; the abstinence period will begin on the 7th day, September 18.

28 − 11 = 17. Therefore, the fertile days will last until the 17th day of the cycle, September 28. The remaining days, from September 29 to the onset of the next menstruation, are sterile once more.

2. Calculation aids

Various aids designed to make easy the calculation of the sterile days can be bought today. Such devices are of no use unless they are simple and accurately indicate the correct days. Unfortunately this cannot be said for some of the aids available.

But even if these aids give the correct days, they achieve their purpose only if the woman in question is well acquainted with her cycle pattern and her sensitivity to disturbances. A calculation aid is of value only when *it is used in conjunction with a reliable book* which gives detailed explanations of the method, or with the assistance of a doctor from whom the woman is receiving regular advice. Most failures arise, in practice, from the fact that married couples are satisfied with a simple formula or a calculation aid, and know nothing of those questions which have received such detailed attention from us in this book. Nature does not allow itself to be compressed into a simple calculation formula or a simple calculation device.

Most readers will certainly find that the tables given in the next section give valuable assistance, especially when used in conjunction with the Chart Sheet and explanation we have added to the book.

One other important point before we explain the tables: in the section which follows the tables we shall comment on the *care* which must be taken when the method is *first being put into practice*.

3. Explanation of the tables for the calculation of the sterile days

The tables which begin on p. 76 constitute a device for immediately ascertaining the date of the abstinence days. All the important cycle patterns have been taken into consideration.

a) *The quintuple cycle pattern*

The tables are intended first for women with quintuple cycle patterns (see Chapter III, §2 e, f). For a cycle pattern of 27–31 days, Table No. 5 must be followed, as the wording of the table indicates.

b) *The triple or quadruple cycle pattern*

As it is unlikely that a triple or quadruple cycle pattern will be maintained in the long run, and probable that continued observation will discover a quintuple pattern, it is better to regard the pattern as quintuple from the beginning and to use the corresponding table.

With triple cycle patterns a day each is added left and right; for example, if up to this a cycle pattern of 28–30 days has been observed, then Table 5 for a cycle pattern of 27–31 days is used.

With quadruple cycle patterns an extra day is added and, as far as possible, in such a way as to make it approximate to a 28-day cycle. If, for example, a cycle pattern of 30–33 days has been observed up to this, Table 7, for the cycle pattern of 29–33 days, is followed. If, in another case, the cycle pattern up to this has been 28–31 days, then Table 5 for the cycle pattern of 27–31 days is used. If, in yet another case, the cycle pattern so far observed has been 24–27 days, Table 2, for the cycle pattern of 24–28 days, is followed.

c) The sextuple and septuple cycle pattern

When the cycle pattern is sextuple or septuple, the table nearest to the quintuple cycle pattern is followed, but an extra day or two is added to the abstinence days shown to compensate for error. For the cycle pattern of 25–30 days, one could use, for example, Table 4 (cycle pattern of 26–30 days), but abstinence would start one day earlier. Examples given further on will help to explain.

For the septuple cycle pattern (26–32 days), Table 5 can be used (cycle pattern of 27–31 days), but an extra day is added to the beginning and the end of the abstinence period.

d) Very short cycles

Women with a cycle pattern of less than 23 days, in actual practice, are able to take advantage of no more than the last 11 days (counted according to the longest cycle), for during the first three or four days sexual relations do not enter into the question in any case because of menstruation. For this reason, only cycle patterns above 23 days have been given in the tables.

e) Arrangement of the tables

The tables have been arranged as follows:

In the first column on the left appear the days of the month from the 1st to 31st. In the next four columns, A, B, C, D, appear the abstinence days. In the first column, on the left, one looks for the day of the month on which menstruation began (not, of course, for the day on which it was expected, but for the actual day when it occurred). For example: menstruation began on September 13. The woman seeks in the first column on the left of her corresponding table the number 13, the date of the onset of menstruation.

In the adjoining four columns (A, B, C, D), she will find the abstinence days for each month of the year, set out as follows:

If the month in which menstruation takes place has 31 days, column A must be consulted.

If the month in which menstruation takes place has 30 days, column B must be consulted.

If the month of February in which menstruation takes place has 28 days, column C must be consulted.

If the month of February in which menstruation takes place has 29 days, column D must be consulted.

Thus the columns will be consulted:

A for the months of January, March, May, July, August, October, December

B for the months of April, June, September, November

C for the month of February with 28 days

D for the month of February with 29 days (1964, 1968, 1972, 1976, 1980, 1984)

So—to return to the example we have already given—this woman whose menstruation has started on September 13 must consult column B, as there are only thirty days in September.

To take another example, the case of a woman whose menstruation begins on April 30 and continues until May 3. She will likewise consult column B, as the month of April, when the bleeding started, has thirty days. May has nothing to do with the matter.

In short: in the date column one looks for the date (the day) of the onset of menstruation; in the corresponding month columns A, B, C, or D (according to the number of days in the month in which menstruation *began*), the abstinence days will be found on the same line.

f) Practical examples

We would like to show, by means of a few examples, how simple and easy to use these tables are.

Example 1. A certain woman has established the following cycles: 32, 34, 31, 32, 35, 31, 33, 32, 31, 39, 35, 33 days. The cycle pattern is 31–35 days (with one exception, 39 days, but this variation is not considered in the determination of the cycle pattern). The last menstruation began on May 11. When are her abstinence days?

This woman will consult Table 9 (cycle pattern of 31–35 days). In the first column on the left, in which the dates of the month from 1 to 31 appear, she will look for the day 11. As the month of May has 31 days she will take column A, for the other columns do not concern her. On the same line as the date 11, she will find the days 23–3 given. This means that, if she wishes to avoid conception, she must abstain from sexual relations from May 23 to June 3. On the remaining days she can have these with an easy mind, that is, from the end of menstruation until May 22, and again from June 4 up to the onset of the next menstruation.

Her menstruation will take place on June 11, 12, 13, 14, or 15. On that day she will once again follow Table 9, and look for the abstinence days applicable to the date of the onset of menstruation, but this time she will look in column B, since the month of June has 30 days; and so on, each month. The abstinence days cannot be calculated several months in advance.

Example 2. As the result of observations a woman has established the following cycles: 25, 27, 20, 23, 24, 25, 26, 25, 24, 23, 27, 25. The last menstruation occurred on February 20, 1961.

She will follow Table 1, cycle pattern of 23–27 days (in spite of the variation of 20 days). 1961 not being a leap year, the month of February has 28 days. Column C must therefore be consulted. Beside the date figure 20 she will find, in column C, the corresponding abstinence days, February 24 to March 7.

Example 3. The cycle pattern is quadruple, 28–31 days. The last menstruation began on April 24. The woman should consult Table 5, "cycle pattern 27–31 days." For the quintuple cycle pattern the abstinence days would extend from May 2 to 13.

Example 4. The cycle pattern is triple, 31–33 days. The last menstruation commenced on June 11. The woman should consult the table for the quintuple cycle pattern, 30–34 days (Table 8). In column B she will find the abstinence days given, June 22 to July 3.

Example 5. A sextuple cycle pattern: 24–29 days. Menstruation began on March 21. Table 2 is consulted for a cycle pattern of 24–28 days, and column A, but an extra day is added. So, instead of March 26 to April 6, one gets March 26 to April 7 for the days of abstinence.

Example 6. A septuple cycle pattern: 25–31 days. The date of menstruation was September 14. Table 4 must be consulted (cycle pattern of 26–30 days). The dates shown in column B are September 21 to October 2. A day is added to each of these, giving the correct reading September 20 to October 3.

Note: It must be understood that these tables are of value only to women with an exact knowledge of their cycle pattern and their susceptibility to disturbance, and who follow the instructions given in the next section.

Ten tables for quintuple cycle patterns between 23 and 36 Days

Table 1

Cycle Pattern: 23-27 Days

Date of first day of menstruation	A	B	C	D
	Dates of the abstinence days when menstruation begins in a month with			
	31 days	30 days	28 days	29 days
1	5-16	5-16	5-16	5-16
2	6-17	6-17	6-17	6-17
3	7-18	7-18	7-18	7-18
4	8-19	8-19	8-19	8-19
5	9-20	9-20	9-20	9-20
6	10-21	10-21	10-21	10-21
7	11-22	11-22	11-22	11-22
8	12-23	12-23	12-23	12-23
9	13-24	13-24	13-24	13-24
10	14-25	14-25	14-25	14-25
11	15-26	15-26	15-26	15-26
12	16-27	16-27	16-27	16-27
13	17-28	17-28	17-28	17-28
14	18-29	18-29	18-1	18-29
15	19-30	19-30	19-2	19-1
16 ·	20-31	20-1	20-3	20-2
17 ·	21-1	21-2	21-4	21-3
18 ·	22-2	22-3	22-5	22-4
19 ´	23-3	23-4	23-6	23-5
20 ·	24-4	24-5	24-7	24-6
21	25-5	25-6	25-8	25-7
22	26-6	26-7	26-9	26-8
23	27-7	27-8	27-10	27-9
24	28-8	28-9	28-11	28-10
25	29-9	29-10	1-12	29-11
26	30-10	30-11	2-13	1-12
27	31-11	1-12	3-14	2-13
28	1-12	2-13	4-15	3-14
29	2-13	3-14		4-15
30	3-14	4-15		
31	4-15			

Table 2

Cycle Pattern: 24-28 Days

Date of first day of menstruation	A	B	C	D
	Dates of the abstinence days when menstruation begins in a month with			
	31 days	30 days	28 days	29 days
1	6-17	6-17	6-17	6-17
2	7-18	7-18	7-18	7-18
3	8-19	8-19	8-19	8-19
4	9-20	9-20	9-20	9-20
5	10-21	10-21	10-21	10-21
6	11-22	11-22	11-22	11-22
7	12-23	12-23	12-23	12-23
8	13-24	13-24	13-24	13-24
9	14-25	14-25	14-25	14-25
10	15-26	15-26	15-26	15-26
11	16-27	16-27	16-27	16-27
12	17-28	17-28	17-28	17-28
13	18-29	18-29	18-1	18-29
14	19-30	19-30	19-2	19-1
15	20-31	20-1	20-3	20-2
16	21-1	21-2	21-4	21-3
17	22-2	22-3	22-5	22-4
18	23-3	23-4	23-6	23-5
19	24-4	24-5	24-7	24-6
20	25-5	25-6	25-8	25-7
21	26-6	26-7	26-9	26-8
22	27-7	27-8	27-10	27-9
23	28-8	28-9	28-11	28-10
24	29-9	29-10	1-12	29-11
25	30-10	30-11	2-13	1-12
26	31-11	1-12	3-14	2-13
27	1-12	2-13	4-15	3-14
28	2-13	3-14	5-16	4-15
29	3-14	4-15		5-16
30	4-15	5-16		
31	5-16			

Table 3

Cycle Pattern: 25-29 Days

Date of first day of menstruation	A	B	C	D
	Dates of the abstinence days when menstruation begins in a month with			
	31 days	30 days	28 days	29 days
1	7-18	7-18	7-18	7-18
2	8-19	8-19	8-19	8-19
3	9-20	9-20	9-20	9-20
4	10-21	10-21	10-21	10-21
5	11-22	11-22	11-22	11-22
6	12-23	12-23	12-23	12-23
7	13-24	13-24	13-24	13-24
8	14-25	14-25	14-25	14-25
9	15-26	15-26	15-26	15-26
10	16-27	16-27	16-27	16-27
11	17-28	17-28	17-28	17-28
12	18-29	18-29	18-1	18-29
13	19-30	19-30	19-2	19-1
14	20-31	20-1	20-3	20-2
15	21-1	21-2	21-4	21-3
16	22-2	22-3	22-5	22-4
17	23-3	23-4	23-6	23-5
18	24-4	24-5	24-7	24-6
19	25-5	25-6	25-8	25-7
20	26-6	26-7	26-9	26-8
21	27-7	27-8	27-10	27-9
22	28-8	28-9	28-11	28-10
23	29-9	29-10	1-12	29-11
24	30-10	30-11	2-13	1-12
25	31-11	1-12	3-14	2-13
26	1-12	2-13	4-15	3-14
27	2-13	3-14	5-16	4-15
28	3-14	4-15	6-17	5-16
29	4-15	5-16		6-17
30	5-16	6-17		
31	6-17			

Table 4

Cycle Pattern: 26-30 Days

Date of first day of menstruation	A	B	C	D
	— Dates of the abstinence days when menstruation begins in a month with			
	31 days	30 days	28 days	29 days
1	8-19	8-19	8-19	8-19
2	9-20	9-20	9-20	9-20
3	10-21	10-21	10-21	10-21
4	11-22	11-22	11-22	11-22
5	12-23	12-23	12-23	12-23
6	13-24	13-24	13-24	13-24
7	14-25	14-25	14-25	14-25
8	15-26	15-26	15-26	15-26
9	16-27	16-27	16-27	16-27
10	17-28	17-28	17-28	17-28
11	18-29	18-29	18-1	18-29
12	19-30	19-30	19-2	19-1
13	20-31	20-1	20-3	20-2
14	21-1	21-2	21-4	21-3
15	22-2	22-3	22-5	22-4
16	23-3	23-4	23-6	23-5
17	24-4	24-5	24-7	24-6
18	25-5	25-6	25-8	25-7
19	26-6	26-7	26-9	26-8
20	27-7	27-8	27-10	27-9
21	28-8	28-9	28-11	28-10
22	29-9	29-10	1-12	29-11
23	30-10	30-11	2-13	1-12
24	31-11	1-12	3-14	2-13
25	1-12	2-13	4-15	3-14
26	2-13	3-14	5-16	4-15
27	3-14	4-15	6-17	5-16
28	4-15	5-16	7-18	6-17
29	5-16	6-17		7-18
30	6-17	7-18		
31	7-18			

Table 5

Cycle Pattern: 27-31 Days

Date of first day of menstruation	A	B	C	D
	Dates of the abstinence days when menstruation begins in a month with			
	31 days	30 days	28 days	29 days
1	9-20	9-20	9-20	9-20
2	10-21	10-21	10-21	10-21
3	11-22	11-22	11-22	11-22
4	12-23	12-23	12-23	12-23
5	13-24	13-24	13-24	13-24
6	14-25	14-25	14-25	14-25
7	15-26	15-26	15-26	15-26
8	16-27	16-27	16-27	16-27
9	17-28	17-28	17-28	17-28
10	18-29	18-29	18-1	18-29
11	19-30	19-30	19-2	19-1
12	20-31	20-1	20-3	20-2
13	21-1	21-2	21-4	21-3
14	22-2	22-3	22-5	22-4
15	23-3	23-4	23-6	23-5
16	24-4	24-5	24-7	24-6
17	25-5	25-6	25-8	25-7
18	26-6	26-7	26-9	26-8
19	27-7	27-8	27-10	27-9
20	28-8	28-9	28-11	28-10
21	29-9	29-10	1-12	29-11
22	30-10	30-11	2-13	1-12
23	31-11	1-12	3-14	2-13
24	1-12	2-13	4-15	3-14
25	2-13	3-14	5-16	4-15
26	3-14	4-15	6-17	5-16
27	4-15	5-16	7-18	6-17
28	5-16	6-17	8-19	7-18
29	6-17	7-18		8-19
30	7-18	8-19		
31	8-19			

Table 6

Cycle Pattern: 28-32 Days

Date of first day of menstruation	A	B	C	D
	Dates of the abstinence days when menstruation begins in a month with			
	31 days	30 days	28 days	29 days
1	10-21	10-21	10-21	10-21
2	11-22	11-22	11-22	11-22
3	12-23	12-23	12-23	12-23
4	13-24	13-24	13-24	13-24
5	14-25	14-25	14-25	14-25
6	15-26	15-26	15-26	15-26
7	16-27	16-27	16-27	16-27
8	17-28	17-28	17-28	17-28
9	18-29	18-29	18-1	18-29
10	19-30	19-30	19-2	19-1
11	20-31	20-1	20-3	20-2
12	21-1	21-2	21-4	21-3
13	22-2	22-3	22-5	22-4
14	23-3	23-4	23-6	23-5
15	24-4	24-5	24-7	24-6
16	25-5	25-6	25-8	25-7
17	26-6	26-7	26-9	26-8
18	27-7	27-8	27-10	27-9
19	28-8	28-9	28-11	28-10
20	29-9	29-10	1-12	29-11
21	30-10	30-11	2-13	1-12
22	31-11	1-12	3-14	2-13
23	1-12	2-13	4-15	3-14
24	2-13	3-14	5-16	4-15
25	3-14	4-15	6-17	5-16
26	4-15	5-16	7-18	6-17
27	5-16	6-17	8-19	7-18
28	6-17	7-18	9-20	8-19
29	7-18	8-19		9-20
30	8-19	9-20		
31	9-20			

Table 7

Cycle Pattern: 29-33 Days

Date of first day of menstruation	A	B	C	D
	Dates of the abstinence days when menstruation begins in a month with			
	31 days	30 days	28 days	29 days
1	11-22	11-22	11-22	11-22
2	12-23	12-23	12-23	12-23
3	13-24	13-24	13-24	13-24
4	14-25	14-25	14-25	14-25
5	15-26	15-26	15-26	15-26
6	16-27	16-27	16-27	16-27
7	17-28	17-28	17-28	17-28
8	18-29	18-29	18-1	18-29
9	19-30	19-30	19-2	19-1
10	20-31	20-1	20-3	20-2
11	21-1	21-2	21-4	21-3
12	22-2	22-3	22-5	22-4
13	23-3	23-4	23-6	23-5
14	24-4	24-5	24-7	24-6
15	25-5	25-6	25-8	25-7
16	26-6	26-7	26-9	26-8
17	27-7	27-8	27-10	27-9
18	28-8	28-9	28-11	28-10
19	29-9	29-10	1-12	29-11
20	30-10	30-11	2-13	1-12
21	31-11	1-12	3-14	2-13
22	1-12	2-13	4-15	3-14
23	2-13	3-14	5-16	4-15
24	3-14	4-15	6-17	5-16
25	4-15	5-16	7-18	6-17
26	5-16	6-17	8-19	7-18
27	6-17	7-18	9-20	8-19
28	7-18	8-19	10-21	9-20
29	8-19	9-20		10-21
30	9-20	10-21		
31	10-21			

Table 8

Cycle Pattern: 30-34 Days

Date of first day of menstruation	A	B	C	D
	Dates of the abstinence days when menstruation begins in a month with			
	31 days	30 days	28 days	29 days
1	12-23	12-23	12-23	12-23
2	13-24	13-24	13-24	13-24
3	14-25	14-25	14-25	14-25
4	15-26	15-26	15-26	15-26
5	16-27	16-27	16-27	16-27
6	17-28	17-28	17-28	17-28
7	18-29	18-29	18-1	18-29
8	19-30	19-30	19-2	19-1
9	20-31	20-1	20-3	20-2
10	21-1	21-2	21-4	21-3
11	22-2	22-3	22-5	22-4
12	23-3	23-4	23-6	23-5
13	24-4	24-5	24-7	24-6
14	25-5	25-6	25-8	25-7
15	26-6	26-7	26-9	26-8
16	27-7	27-8	27-10	27-9
17	28-8	28-9	28-11	28-10
18	29-9	29-10	1-12	29-11
19	30-10	30-11	2-13	1-12
20	31-11	1-12	3-14	2-13
21	1-12	2-13	4-15	3-14
22	2-13	3-14	5-16	4-15
23	3-14	4-15	6-17	5-16
24	4-15	5-16	7-18	6-17
25	5-16	6-17	8-19	7-18
26	6-17	7-18	9-20	8-19
27	7-18	8-19	10-21	9-20
28	8-19	9-20	11-22	10-21
29	9-20	10-21		11-22
30	10-21	11-22		
31	11-22			

Table 9

Cycle Pattern: 31-35 Days

Date of first day of menstruation	A	B	C	D
	Dates of the abstinence days when menstruation begins in a month with			
	31 days	30 days	28 days	29 days
1	13-24	13-24	13-24	13-24
2	14-25	14-25	14-25	14-25
3	15-26	15-26	15-26	15-26
4	16-27	16-27	16-27	16-27
5	17-28	17-28	17-28	17-28
6	18-29	18-29	18-1	18-29
7	19-30	19-30	19-2	19-1
8	20-31	20-1	20-3	20-2
9	21-1	21-2	21-4	21-3
10	22-2	22-3	22-5	22-4
11	23-3	23-4	23-6	23-5
12	24-4	24-5	24-7	24-6
13	25-5	25-6	25-8	25-7
14	26-6	26-7	26-9	26-8
15	27-7	27-8	27-10	27-9
16	28-8	28-9	28-11	28-10
17	29-9	29-10	1-12	29-11
18	30-10	30-11	2-13	1-12
19	31-11	1-12	3-14	2-13
20	1-12	2-13	4-15	3-14
21	2-13	3-14	5-16	4-15
22	3-14	4-15	6-17	5-16
23	4-15	5-16	7-18	6-17
24	5-16	6-17	8-19	7-18
25	6-17	7-18	9-20	8-19
26	7-18	8-19	10-21	9-20
27	8-19	9-20	11-22	10-21
28	9-20	10-21	12-23	11-22
29	10-21	11-22		12-23
30	11-22	12-23		
31	12-23			

Table 10

Cycle Pattern: 32-36 Days

Date of first day of menstruation	A	B	C	D
	Dates of the abstinence days when menstruation begins in a month with			
	31 days	30 days	28 days	29 days
1	14-25	14-25	14-25	14-25
2	15-26	15-26	15-26	15-26
3	16-27	16-27	16-27	16-27
4	17-28	17-28	17-28	17-28
5	18-29	18-29	18-1	18-29
6	19-30	19-30	19-2	19-1
7	20-31	20-1	20-3	20-2
8	21-1	21-2	21-4	21-3
9	22-2	22-3	22-5	22-4
10	23-3	23-4	23-6	23-5
11	24-4	24-5	24-7	24-6
12	25-5	25-6	25-8	25-7
13	26-6	26-7	26-9	26-8
14	27-7	27-8	27-10	27-9
15	28-8	28-9	28-11	28-10
16	29-9	29-10	1-12	29-11
17	30-10	30-11	2-13	1-12
18	31-11	1-12	3-14	2-13
19	1-12	2-13	4-15	3-14
20	2-13	3-14	5-16	4-15
21	3-14	4-15	6-17	5-16
22	4-15	5-16	7-18	6-17
23	5-16	6-17	8-19	7-18
24	6-17	7-18	9-20	8-19
25	7-18	8-19	10-21	9-20
26	8-19	9-20	11-22	10-21
27	9-20	10-21	12-23	11-22
28	10-21	11-22	13-24	12-23
29	11-22	12-23		13-24
30	12-23	13-24		
31	13-24			

4. The practical application of the method in order to avoid conception

a) The procedure during the observation period

Even if the exact cycle pattern is not yet known, one must at least be aware of the approximate duration of the cycle. It is taken for granted that every woman knows this, but, if she does not, she must carry out observations for two to three months, and she must abstain from sexual relations during this period. Then it is assumed that the following month the cycle will have the same duration, although this is by no means certain. Calculating back from the date of the next expected menstruation, five days only will be regarded as safe (the last five days before the expected onset of the next menstruation). During the rest of the time, abstinence will be practiced. This precaution must be taken until the cycle pattern is known exactly.

Example: A woman knows that her cycle pattern shows no great variations and lasts approximately a month. Her last menstruation was on March 19; therefore, her next menstruation should occur about April 19. Consequently she practices abstinence until April 14 and resumes sexual relations on April 15. Menstruation begins unexpectedly on April 17; her cycle has had a duration of only 29 days. If her next cycle has also a duration of only 29 days, the next menstruation will occur on May 16. But as she cannot be certain of this, she will regard only the five last days before this date—May 11 to 15—as being safe for sexual relations. She will continue to act thus until such time as she has an exact knowledge of the duration of her cycles. (See Fig. 28.)

May 9	10	11	12	13	14	15	16
		5	4	3	2	1	
Abstinence days				Safe days			Probable start of menstruation

Fig. 28

It is obviously imperative to be able, with the aid of the temperature chart or the glucose test, to determine the time of ovulation as accurately as possible. We shall say more of this in subsection c below.

b) *When the cycle pattern is known exactly*

As we already know, the essential condition for the employment of the method of periodic abstinence in order to avoid conception is that every woman must have an exact knowledge of her cycle peculiarities. She must know:

1. Which cycle pattern she has. She must have noted the length of her cycles for a period of at least one year, and she must, on the basis of the longest and shortest cycle, know their margin of variation.

2. Although the margin of variation so far observed may not have exceeded three or four days, she must nevertheless consider herself to have *at least a quintuple pattern*, as we have already explained in §3 b of this chapter.

3. If there is uncertainty as to when the cycles actually begin, and if it is difficult to distinguish the onset of menstruation —due to the occurrence of bleeding which one does not know whether or not to be the expected menstruation—the start and end of the cycle can be easily determined by a regular recording of the temperature. As we have already said in Chapter II, §2 b, the temperature falls at the beginning of the cycle. (See Fig. 4.)

4. On the basis of observations over a period of months or years a woman must, as we have said in Chapter IV, §2, know her sensitivity to disturbances. In some women, outside happenings produce practically no disturbance in their cycles, but others, especially those of nervous disposition and of unstable hormonal balance, are very susceptible to disturbance and must take this into account in calculating the sterile days. To cycles in which an event has occurred which is liable to alter the ovulation or menstruation times—such as a severe nervous shock,

a change of climate, unusually strenuous activity, etc.—the general rule does not apply. In §4 d of this chapter we shall deal with the course to be followed in such cases.

Even those women who have always carefully observed the pattern of their cycles, and whose lengths they know accurately, should nevertheless be cautious in their initial application of the method, for sexual relations themselves—admittedly very rarely—can be among the causes liable to produce a change in the cycle pattern.

Furthermore, the gradual introduction of the method has a reassuring effect on those of timid disposition. Worry and anxiety often cause cycle disturbances and delay the onset of menstruation.

It would, consequently, be unwise at the beginning to make use of all the sterile days. During the first months, married couples should add a few abstinence days; abstinence should be practiced one, two, or three days earlier than the date given by calculation or the tables, and should continue from one to three days longer than the stipulated date.

If it is possible, engaged couples should arrange the date of their marriage so that sexual relations would begin about a week before the onset of the next expected menstruation.

Married couples should proceed for a few months with the caution previously described and constantly and accurately observe and note the cycle lengths. After a time they will know whether the cycle pattern changes as a result of sexual relations and which pattern it has assumed. The experience thus acquired will give them an essential feeling of security.

At the beginning it is best to make use of the last 5 to 7 days only (always counting back from the longest cycle), then the last 7 to 9 days, finally the last 11 days, and even the days following menstruation. The question of how quickly all the sterile days can be utilized depends on the behavior of the woman's cycle pattern under the influence of sexual relations. The more regular are the cycles, the fewer the abstinence days that are necessary and the more days that can be utilized; the more irregular are the cycles, the more cautious must one be.

The same caution (as mentioned above) should be observed if, for whatever reason—voluntary abstinence, separation consequent upon illness, pregnancy, etc.—sexual relations have been interrupted for a fairly long period. The conditions most favorable for the successful implementation of the method are that the married couple should lead a steady, regular life together and should avoid any drastic change in their mode of living or their diet.

c) When definite exterior symptoms of ovulation are determined

According to Dr. Holt, 75 per cent of women are capable of recognizing those exterior ovulation symptoms—of which we have spoken in Chapter II, §2—provided that they have learned to observe them.

The correct observation of the ovulation symptoms makes it easier to determine the abstinence days and is, therefore, especially important when cycles are very varied, or irregular, or disturbed.

For the determination of the sterile days one observes the following instructions:

During the first months such symptoms as the intermenstrual pain, or a characteristic mucous discharge, a slight bleeding, or a swelling and tenseness of the breasts will be only observed and accurately noted in a menstrual calendar (Chapter IV, §3). When menstruation occurs, one can satisfy oneself, by reckoning back, whether the symptom in question was actually an ovulation symptom. If it was observed about two weeks before the start of menstruation, it can be regarded as a definite symptom of ovulation.

In the case of the intermenstrual pain, one should also try to observe whether it occurs alternately on the left and on the right side, as ovulation normally takes place in the right ovary and left ovary alternately. The intermenstrual pain lasts—sometimes with intervals of hours at a time—for one or two days.

When it has vanished completely, 3 *full days* (as recommended by Dr. Holt) must be allowed to elapse. Then as soon as it is certain that the pain observed was indeed the intermenstrual pain, one can safely have sexual intercourse after these three days without fear of pregnancy.

With other ovulation symptoms also, such as mucous discharges or slight bleedings, intercourse must be delayed until three days after they have disappeared. In the same way, intercourse can take place safely three days after the appearance of the typical swelling of the breasts.

The woman who regularly measures her temperature in the specified manner, and observes the sudden rise in the temperature curve, indicative of ovulation, likewise can resume intercourse three days later without fear of conception.

It can only be established with certainty that ovulation has taken place and that the sterile days have already begun if, for three consecutive days—and on each of these three days—the temperature is *higher* than on any other day in the preceding week or, at least, than on any of the five preceding days. An example will help to explain this:

A woman has recorded the following daily temperatures: 97.8°, 97.7°, 97.7°, 97.8°, 97.7°, 97.1°, 98.7°, 98.6°, and 98.9°. During the last three days the temperature has remained above even the highest temperature recorded on any of the six preceding days. We are not primarily concerned with *how high* the temperature is but only that it should be *higher* than any of the temperatures of the preceding week. In connection with this, one should once more turn to the chart of the temperature curve (see Fig. 4).

The delay of three days after recognized ovulation symptoms is considered essential in order to avoid miscalculation and errors.

A similar caution should be exercised with the glucose test. When the test shows that ovulation has already taken place, three more days must be allowed to elapse and the test must be repeated daily. If, on the next two days, a faint color appears but, on the third day after ovulation, no further sign of color can be detected, one can almost be certain that conception is impossible during the remaining days of the cycle. This precaution is essential in order to avoid mistakes, for the first observation of color could be due to some other cause.

It would be wrong to assume that calculation, the so-called calendar method, has become superfluous and that one may now rely on the temperature chart and the glucose test. The calculation method remains, as before, the foundation of periodic abstinence and is at present the sole method by which the period of the sterile days at the beginning of the cycle can be determined.

The importance of the temperature chart and the glucose test lies in the fact that, with their aid, the start of the last 11 days can be determined with greater ease and accuracy even in disturbed cycles and in special cases, such as after childbirth, etc. (see Chapter VII).

d) *The procedure when the cycles are affected by disturbing influences*

We have already mentioned (Chapter III) that even in healthy women with a constant cycle pattern, strong exterior influences, of a physical or psychological nature, can at times cause disturbances in the cycle. Consequently, it is very important that every woman should regularly and accurately observe her susceptibility to disturbance, and know her reactions. The entries in the menstrual calendar help her in this. We have already said, too, that the effects of these disturbing influences are different according to the particular phase of the cycle in which they occur.

What should a woman do if, as a result of an accident, for example, or unusual overwork or a serious fright, she is afraid that her cycle has been disturbed?

If the disturbance occurs in the *second half* of the cycle, when ovulation has already taken place, the answer is very simple. No special precaution is necessary and there is no cause for worry, even if the menstruation is a little delayed. (See Fig. 29.)

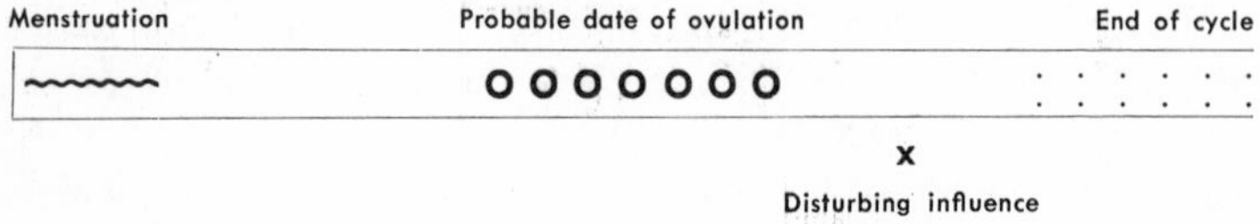

Menstruation	Probable date of ovulation	End of cycle
~~	O O O O O O O	· · · · · · ·
		· · · · · · ·

X

Disturbing influence

Fig. 29

The next cycles will probably be normal again. As a precautionary measure, however, a longer period of abstinence is observed in the next cycle, an extra two days being added to the beginning and end respectively. Example: cycle pattern of 27–31 days; normal abstinence period: 9th to 20th day; prolonged abstinence period: 7th to 22nd day. (See Fig. 30.)

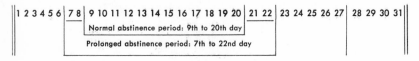

Fig. 30.   Cycle pattern of 27 to 31 days

Should the disturbing influence occur in the first part of the cycle, so that there is a danger of the ovulation date being upset, great caution is necessary—the abstinence period must be extended by at least a week, or intercourse put off until after the next menstruation. (See Fig. 31.)

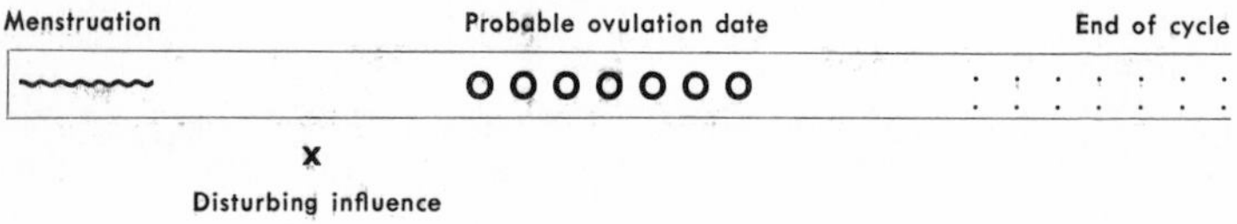

Menstruation	Probable ovulation date	End of cycle
~~	O O O O O O O	· · · · · · ·
		· · · · · · ·

X

Disturbing influence

Fig. 31

Example: A woman has a cycle pattern of 27–31 days, with a normal abstinence period from the 9th to the 20th day of the cycle. She meets with an accident on the 8th day of the cycle. As one cannot tell whether or not the emotional shock will retard ovulation, the abstinence period will be prolonged until the 27th day. If the cycle shows no sign of disturbance, the normal pattern of behavior will be followed in the course of the next cycle; but if it shows itself to be abnormal, two days are added to the abstinence period as a precautionary measure.

Attention is once more drawn to the fact that in all doubtful and difficult cases observation of ovulation symptoms and of the temperature, or the use of the glucose test, can be a great help.

If the cycle breaks off abruptly and if (false) menstruation occurs two weeks before the expected date, as a result of a disturbing accident having taken place at *ovulation* time, caution must be exercised in the course of the next cycle and the abstinence period prolonged by two days, as described before. (See Fig. 32.)

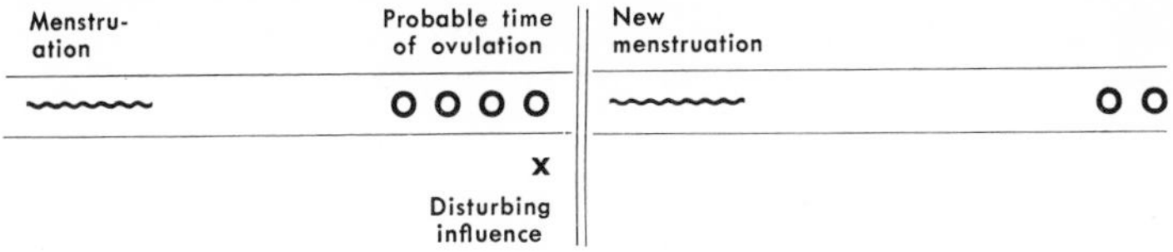

Menstru- ation	Probable time of ovulation	New menstruation
~~	o o o o	~~~~ o o
	x Disturbing influence	

Fig. 32

If no premature bleeding follows the disturbing influence at ovulation time, then *total abstinence* must be observed until *menstruation returns*. If this does not take place at the normal time, corresponding to the known pattern of the cycle, the abstinence period will be prolonged by an extra two days in the following month. (See Fig. 33.)

When a disturbing event occurs during the ovulation days, *complete abstinence* must be observed *in every case* until the new cycle begins, even if ovulation symptoms have been observed. For a cycle often ceases abruptly and unobserved, and a

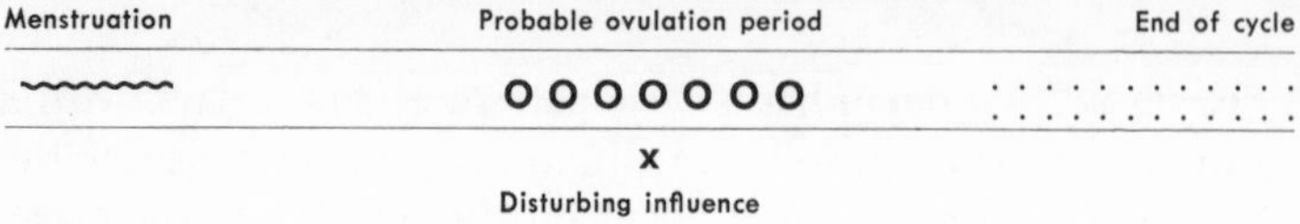

Menstruation	Probable ovulation period	End of cycle
∿∿∿	O O O O O O O	· · · · · · · · · · · · ·
	X	
	Disturbing influence	

Fig. 33

new cycle begins *without* menstruation. This is the type of case which, in practice, presents the most difficulty. (See Fig. 34.)

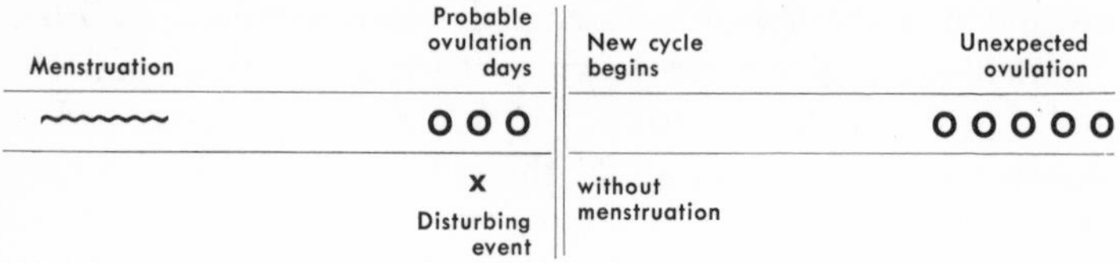

Menstruation	Probable ovulation days	New cycle begins	Unexpected ovulation
∿∿∿	O O O		O O O O O
	X Disturbing event	without menstruation	

Fig. 34

Specialist opinion remains open on the question whether conception is likely when the ovulation period is upset. Ogino believed that the ovum lost its fertility when, as a result of some disturbing event, it was not expelled at the normal time. On the other hand, Knaus and Holt advise only greater caution.

Slight variations of some two to three days in the ovulation period need not give rise to worry, for allowance has already been made for them in the general rule of abstinence (see Chapter II, §4 and §6).

e) *Changes in the cycle pattern*

When the cycle pattern varies, purely as a result of the *natural undulatory movement* and without any outside cause therefor being recognized, this circumstance will be taken into consideration in calculating the abstinence days which correspond to the new cycle pattern. This must again be at least quintuple.

On the other hand, if a variation in the whole cycle pattern occurs as the result of a known cause—for example, a change of climate, or great psychological suffering (resulting from a very severe shock or such like), or a change in the way of living (dietary or so forth)—the old as well as the new cycle pattern must be considered when the sterile days are being calculated, because the old cycle pattern may come back at any time as soon as the disturbing element ceases to have effect. A longer abstinence period must be observed, just as though the two cycle patterns were present at the same time. Example: the earlier cycle pattern was 27–31 days; the variation has given the cycle a pattern of 29–33 days. The abstinence days are calculated in accordance with a cycle pattern of 27–33 days, and these days will be adhered to until a new cycle pattern is clearly discernible. The temperature chart and the glucose test help to produce clarification.

5. When procreation is desired

a) The most favorable days for conception

We have already stated in Chapter II, §4 that the possibility of fertilization exists from the 12th to the 19th day before the start of the next menstruation. But the likelihood of fertilization is not equally great on all of these days; the probability of conception is greatest from the 15th to the 17th day before the start of the next menstruation (see Fig. 35).

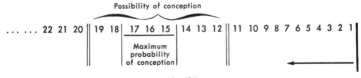

Fig. 35

Example: A woman with a cycle pattern of 31–35 days wishes to find the most favorable days for conception; the last menstruation began on November 9. This woman's fertile days are from November 21 to December 2 (Table 9). The probability of conception is less during the first two and last three days of this period, so the days of maximum probability are from November 23 to 29.

b) Preparation for procreation

For procreation, the day or days chosen from the woman's fertile period should be those on which both partners, psychologically and physically, are best disposed to it.

Specialists are divided in their views upon the extent of the damage wrought by alcohol on the seminal cells. Dr. R. Fetscher, a university professor, in his book *Alkoholfrage in der Vererbung*, published by Neuland-Verlag, Berlin-Hamburg, 1934, wrote that it would be foolish to ignore the possibility of alcohol being harmful to the seminal cells. Fetscher relied principally upon the investigations which Dr. Agnes Bluhm carried out at the Kaiser-Wilhelm Institute of Biology, Berlin, "which allow us to declare today with certainty that through poisons acting directly on the seminal cells, such as alcohol, permanent damage can be done to the hereditary make-up."

It may well be imagined what harm can be caused if the seminal cells, which contain in embryo the hereditary traits of the child, are poisoned. And the most disastrous and appalling consequence of all is that the injustice done to the child can never be rectified.

The responsible act of procreation must naturally be shielded from everything harmful to it. Neither the father nor the mother should be in any way intoxicated or infected at the time of procreation. Not only alcohol but all narcotics, such as nicotine, morphine, cocaine, etc., damage the seminal cells. Intercourse should be postponed if one of the partners is suffering from a venereal disease (syphilis, gonorrhea), or is in the first stage of tuberculosis; it should be postponed in cases of slight or severe feverish illness (influenza), at times of great fatigue, of physical or psychological exhaustion, after profound mental agitation or shock, and even after a too ample meal. Certain occupational diseases, such as lead, mercurial, or nicotine poisoning, and also accidental poisoning (by arsenic, salicylic acid, iodine, bromine, chlorine, strychnine, etc.) have a damaging effect on the seminal cells.

One should also avoid procreation during the time when·one is undergoing X-ray therapy. The sexual glands of husband and wife should not, as far as possible, be exposed to this treatment, for these rays can bring about enduring changes in hereditary factors which can produce in the offspring erratic changes, malformations (so-called mutations). Admittedly the danger of a malformation in the offspring arises only if the father *and* mother have sustained such damage. The rays liberated by atomic energy are substantially more dangerous.

A doctor should be consulted in all instances where it is feared that the seminal cells have been damaged. In accordance with his advice, the couple should postpone procreation until they are again in good health.

If the married pair cannot, or will not, dispense with a honeymoon trip, with its attendant excitements, exertions and fatigues, they should at least avoid conception during this time and confine sexual relations to the sterile days.

During the last weeks before procreation, the couple should see to it that their diet is a health-giving one (fruit and plenty of vegetables), that no alcohol is taken, and that smoking is given up or at least cut down. They should also avoid overindulgence in sports or sexual relations in order to conserve energy. The best psychological preparation in the natural order is the deep love that each partner bears for the other. Religious couples will not neglect spiritual preparation either.

c) *Absence of pregnancy and miscarriage*

During pregnancy and nursing, the woman must carefully avoid all those things designated as harmful, for they can injure the child unborn or at the breast. Some toxins can induce premature birth or miscarriage. During pregnancy, women with a tendency to miscarriages should regularly take their waking temperature. Should this fall, they should consult the doctor without delay.

Intercourse during the days already indicated will very probably result in pregnancy, even in cases where husband and wife have previously been forced to avoid conception over a long period.

If the wished-for conception does not take place, the woman should take accurate temperature readings throughout several cycles in the manner described in Chapter II and in Chapter IV, §4, and show the chart to her doctor. He will be able to see from it whether, perhaps, a fault in the ovulation rhythm is responsible for the sterility to date. The glucose test can, of course, be used in place of temperature reading.

The position of the internal sexual organs of the woman and various other causes can make conception difficult.

The husband and wife must always undergo a medical examination in order to discover the cause of undesired childlessness. If the cause of the childlessness is simply that intercourse is not being practiced at the right time, the glucose test can help to determine the ovulation period accurately.

Procreation is something so noble and so full of responsibility that one should prepare oneself for it in a spirit of dedicated endeavor.

d) Boy or girl?

As far back as the First World War, in order to determine on which days of her menstrual cycle a woman is capable of conception, various doctors collected the dates on which women became pregnant during their husbands' short leave periods. We know today that their investigation methods were wrong, and so it is not surprising that their extensive researches achieved no useful result but, on the contrary, were the source of serious misunderstandings.

It is appalling and tragic to find even today opponents of Knaus depending on these unscientific statistics. They make the mistake of failing to differentiate between a statistical frequency law and an individual biological law. As an answer to the question of the conception date, these statistics—upon which we have already spoken in Chapter V, §3—consequently were, and are, worthless.

Those particular specialists wanted to find the answer to another question in the course of their investigations among the wives of soldiers on furlough: What influence has the time of conception on the sex of the child? And it is remarkable that they all arrived at the same conclusion, namely, that most of the boys were conceived at the start of the cycle, most of the girls only in the last phase of the cycle, around the third week.

Rightly interpreted and rightly expressed—and in so far as the observations made were sufficiently accurate—these findings have the following significance only: The shorter the cycle of a particular woman, the greater the probability of a boy being born; the longer the cycle of a particular woman, the greater the probability of a girl being born.

At first sight, such a conclusion seems to be in opposition to established scientific findings, for it is known that the masculine spermatozoon responsible for fertilization determines and brings with it, so to speak, the sex of the child. This apparent contradiction is easily explained.

It must be assumed that the female organism makes a natural biochemical selection from the injected spermatozoa. This choice is probably decided by the different degree of ionization, or, to use the scientific expression, by the pH count of the female secretions with which the spermatozoon comes in contact.

The decisive influence is probably exercised by the fluid discharged from the follicle upon the release of the ovum. It is received by the oviduct and flows on into the uterus, where it acts simply as a signpost for the spermatozoa present. Presumably the biochemical composition of this follicular fluid varies slightly in accordance with the length of time taken by the follicle to reach maturity.

If, therefore, a married couple wish to have a boy, they should have intercourse during the period from the 5th to the 10th day of the cycle and then abstain until the sterile days toward the end of the cycle. If ovulation does not take place by the 11th day at the latest, no conception will occur during that cycle, but if it takes place on time, conception is almost certain and the child will most probably be a boy.

If the parents want to have a girl, they must practice abstinence until the 16th day of the cycle, then they should resume intercourse until the end of the cycle. If ovulation has already taken place, there will be no conception, but if conception does occur, owing to the fact that the cycle has been a long one, the child will probably be a girl. (See Fig. 36.)

5	6	7	8	9	10	11	12	13	14	15	16	17	18	19	20	21	22	23	...
		Boys				?	?	?	?	?				Girls					

Fig. 36

We are not able at present to say anything in respect of the probable sex of a child conceived between the 10th and 16th day. The fact that there are twins of both sexes shows, in any case, that the female organism does not always make a completely unequivocal choice from among the injected spermatozoa. There must be a period of gradual transition which probably lies between the 10th and the 16th day of the cycle.

The spermatozoon carries the sex, but—according to this theory—it is the female organism which decides, mostly or solely, which spermatozoon penetrates to the ovum and fertilizes it. Through the undulatory movement of the cycle patterns (Chapter III, §4) around the 28-day cycle, which seems to represent the turning point between boys and girls, nature apparently strives to strike a balance between the number of boys and girls.

The theory of the decisive influence exercised by the maternal organism on the sex of the child through her selection from among the "suitor" spermatozoa has not so far been recognized by science, since the whole question has as yet been insufficiently investigated and the science of the cycle is still in its infancy.

In any event, we should like to see further discussion and investigation of this question. So far as our own, not very extensive, practical experience goes, our theory is confirmed by results. It is difficult to extract from scientific publications either confirmation or refutation, because the data are too inexact. The exception is the Smulders-Holt-Heymeijer, *Periodieke Onthouding in het Huwelijk* (Periodic Continence and Marriage) (7th ed., Utrecht, 1934), which provides in every case the dates of the cycle and the sex of the child. The cases described therein seem to confirm the correctness of our theory.

VII

PROCEDURE IN SPECIAL CASES

1. After childbirth

It is very important to avoid conception directly after a birth, for a fresh pregnancy, coming in close succession to the last, would have a weakening effect on the female organism. When the mother is not breast feeding the child, the first menstruation usually occurs very soon—about six weeks—after the confinement. A fresh pregnancy, therefore, could begin as early as a month after childbirth.

Again, when the mother is only partly breast feeding her child and when the mother's milk is being supplemented by other food, menstruation usually reappears soon.

When the mother is entirely breast feeding her child, menstruation usually ceases for a very long time—five to six months.

The first three or four cycles after a birth generally last for a long period, from 40 to 50 days. Then by degrees the original cycle pattern reappears or, at least, one very little different from it. Sometimes, after a certain space of time, a longer cycle appears even though it has been preceded by one or two cycles of the habitual duration. Figure 37 is an example (according to Professor Knaus).

This is why it is difficult to determine the abstinence days after

102

a birth. Observation of the ovulation symptoms and, particularly, the temperature chart can be of assistance.

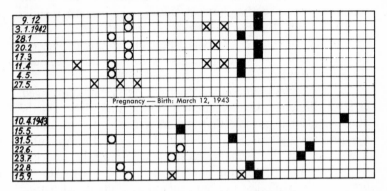

Fig. 37. In the column of dates, the day of the month is given first, followed by the *month*

During the lactation period there sometimes occur cycles without ovulation, in which conception is impossible. Advantage cannot be taken of this, however, because such cycles are not known in advance, although they can be recognized by observation of the temperature on waking or by the glucose test.

Dr. Smulders gives as a *general rule:* During the first cycles, which will probably be long, the first 7 or 8 days are suitable for intercourse. Then one waits for at least 26 days, from the 9th to the 34th day of the cycle.

A child should not be weaned during the first phase of the cycle, before ovulation, for this could completely upset the time of ovulation, thereby throwing the cycles into disorder again. Weaning must take place *toward the end of the cycle.*

When a woman has observed at least three consecutive cycles to be of habitual length, she can gradually return to her normal calculation, utilizing at first only the presumed last five days, then the last eight days, and finally all the sterile days. It is much easier to determine the sterile days by observation of the temperature curve or by the glucose test.

2. After a miscarriage

If a woman suffers a miscarriage, it is essential for her to consult her doctor, so that he may decide whether she requires aftertreatment. The first menstruation generally comes within four to six weeks after a miscarriage. During this period, out of consideration for the woman's health, sexual intercourse should be avoided.

The first cycles after a miscarriage as a rule are not prolonged, as after childbirth, because there is no breast feeding. On the other hand, it is possible that they may not quite conform to the previous pattern and that disturbances and irregularities may arise. On this account, great caution must be exercised from the start in the determination of the sterile days. In the first cycle, only the last five days should be utilized, calculating back from the longest cycle. If no unusual irregularities or variations occur, more and more safe days can be utilized. As soon as the old cycle pattern is found to have returned, the old rule applies again, just as before pregnancy. If a variation has arisen, the correct days must be freshly calculated, as we have shown in Chapter VI, §4 e.

If the waking temperature is regularly observed or the glucose test is performed, the number of abstinence days could very probably be reduced.

3. After a serious illness

In all cases where illness has affected sexual activity or conjugal life, the fundamental rule is to follow absolutely the advice of the doctor in charge. As the cycle pattern can change during convalescence following upon an illness, one begins, unless the doctor has otherwise prescribed, with the last five days (always calculating back from the longest cycle) and then slowly and cautiously progresses toward the gradual utilization of all the remaining sterile days.

Provided that the temperature of the body is normal, observation of the temperature can most positively facilitate the determination of the days of abstinence. The glucose test also can help considerably.

4. In cases of chronic disease

When an impending pregnancy would gravely threaten the woman's health, it is essential that a medical specialist be asked to calculate the sterile days. As a general direction the following can be stated:

It cannot be assumed with any certainty that in sick women the organic processes take place with the same regular rhythm as in those who are healthy. Dependent upon the nature of the disease, it is not certain that menstruation will always occur between the 12th and 16th day after ovulation. Variations resulting from the illness must be anticipated, and consequently more abstinence days must be observed than in the case of healthy women (unless the doctor considers it unnecessary). And so, the abstinence period should start *4 days earlier* and extend *2 days longer*.

Example: A woman, whose health would be seriously endangered by a fresh pregnancy, expects her menstruation between August 25 and 29. Had she been in good health, the abstinence days for her would be from August 6 to 17. Because of her illness, she will begin to practice abstinence 4 days earlier (on August 2), and will add 2 extra days (August 18 and 19). So her abstinence period will be from August 2 to 19 (see Fig. 38).

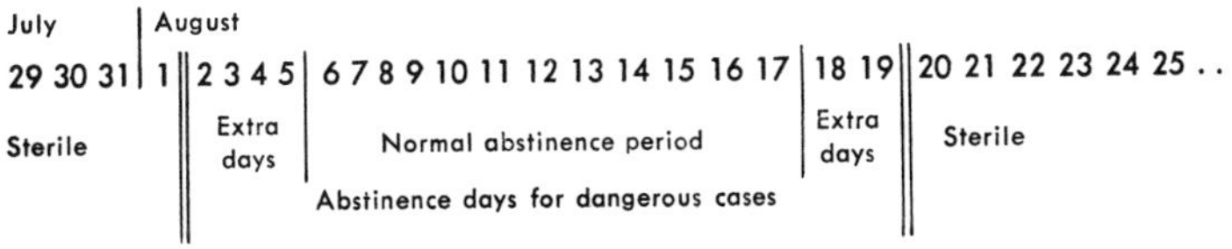

July	August				
29 30 31	1	2 3 4 5	6 7 8 9 10 11 12 13 14 15 16 17	18 19	20 21 22 23 24 25 ..
Sterile		Extra days	Normal abstinence period	Extra days	Sterile
			Abstinence days for dangerous cases		

Fig. 38

The doctor must be the judge as to whether observation of the waking temperature facilitates determination of the sterile days, because the temperature of the body can be so affected by the illness as to make it impossible to recognize the ovulation time from the temperature curve. The glucose test could probably help.

5. In irregular cycle patterns

The application of the foregoing method is scarcely practicable in cases where there is general irregularity in the onset of menstruation, where, for instance, a woman has no menstruation for months and then has a mixture of cycles from 14 to 36 days. A doctor should be consulted in each individual case. It is possible to determine the ovulation period through regular temperature readings, or as the result of other signs, and especially through the glucose test.

6. Procedure when undergoing medical treatment, or change of climate

An abnormal cycle pattern will be produced artificially, so to speak, by the intake of certain *hormone preparations* or other medicines which the gynecologist must sometimes prescribe. Hormones derived from the pituitary glands (especially prolan) or from those of the ovaries (folliculin or progesterone), or from the thyroid gland (thyroxin) are extremely likely to bring about changes in the cycle.

The female organism usually reacts in the same way to other changes in the mode of life—for example, a slimming regimen or other special diets, such as a change to uncooked or purely vegetarian food, and finally to a prolonged change of climate, particularly with differences in altitude, or visits to faraway places with big differences in timekeeping (Europe-America, for example).

In all these cases it is hardly possible to calculate ovulation time in advance with sufficient accuracy, especially at the start of the change or of the treatment. A certain amount of time is needed in order to observe how the cycle reacts to the new situation. In the beginning, therefore, only the last 5 days—calculating back from the longest cycle hitherto observed—can be utilized. With increasing clarification of the new development of the cycle pattern, the days may be added to gradually.

Observation of the temperature curve, and other ovulation symptoms, as well as the use of the glucose test, can help substantially. Your doctor should always be consulted, also.

7. Procedure during the change of life

It is frequently put forward that pregnancy cannot take place during the change of life (climacteric). This is not quite accurate. Although it is an extremely rare occurrence, a woman can become pregnant during this period.

As the cycles are generally very irregular at this time, it is not possible to give universally safe advice as to behavior. The advice of a doctor together with *observation of ovulation symptoms* is recommended.

Self-application of the method, without medical advice, does not afford complete security during the change of life. To those who are prepared to accept some risk of pregnancy, the following general direction may serve: If the cycles are usually very long, the first days after menstruation can be availed of for sexual intercourse. If, on the contrary, the cycles are generally short, it is better to make use only of the presumed last eight or five days.

As a general rule, a woman becomes permanently sterile a few years before the cessation of menstruation, but the judgment of the doctor must be accepted in every individual case.

There occur cycles without ovulation which can be recognized with the assistance of the temperature chart (Chapter II, §2 b), or the glucose test (Chapter IV, §5).

VIII

TO AVOID FAILURE

1. Medical consultation

The statement has often been made that the method of periodic abstinence should be applied only under the direction of
a doctor, on the grounds that when married couples calculate
the fertile and sterile days themselves, without medical assistance, the danger of error is much too great.

First of all it must be pointed out that, unfortunately, this
requirement is not workable in practice because there are always too few doctors qualified to advise married couples correctly.

When the method was in its infancy, it was often attacked.
In a long chapter of his book, *Die Physiologie der Zeugung des
Menschen*, Professor Knaus joined issue with his opponents and
completely exposed the untenableness of the objections. The
reason for the many wrong views was, in nearly all cases, the
fact that, as a result of an erroneous belief in a 28-day normal
cycle, the trouble had not been taken to observe correctly the
actual cycle pattern of the woman in question and her susceptibility to disturbances.

The objections raised against Knaus's teaching, although
positively incorrect, have made many doctors wary of it. They

108

do not believe in this method, although its full exposition is very easily procured, especially from the book by Knaus just mentioned and also by the study of the numerous examples in practical experiments which have been described at length in books by Smulders, Holt, and Stecher.

There are other doctors who regard the method with indifference. The scruples of Christian married couples are beyond their comprehension, and they prefer to prescribe the use of unnatural contraceptive methods because these are simpler in their application than the observation of cycles and calculation of days.

Still small, indeed, is the number of those doctors who have devoted serious attention to the method, its possibilities, and its difficulties. Those who have done so have had excellent results without exception. We furnish numerous proofs of this in the next chapter of this book.

Lastly, many doctors, without preconceived opinions and who view the new method sympathetically, feel that they were not sufficiently instructed at medical school in all aspects of the question. Later it is difficult for them to gather practical experience because there usually come to their consulting rooms only difficult cases—women who, on medical grounds, must avoid pregnancy at all costs. Add to this the fact that practically none of these women has kept an accurate note of her cycles and her sensitivity to disturbances (menstruation calendar, see Chapter IV). The determination of the ovulation time with the aid of the temperature chart is in many cases not possible with these sick women because the body temperature has become affected by the illness. Hence a doctor who has had no practical experience of the method other than in difficult cases can do nothing but advise a lengthy abstinence period.

To give young doctors ample opportunity to gather data, it would be necessary for health authorities and clinics to set up consultation for healthy women as well, and that these centers be placed under the direction of experienced physicians. Most healthy women probably would not attend such centers. In this there is nothing either to wonder at or condemn. Today, in nearly all walks of life from the cradle to the grave, man must live according to directions and regulations issued by official and semiofficial authorities, organizations and institutions, indeed even by the advertising departments of manufacturers of consumer-goods, who direct, advise, provide—always knowing better than he what is good for him. Must he also surrender the last portion of his personal autonomy and submit himself to control and guidance—even though it be of a medical nature—in the most intimate sphere of married life? Conjugal relations are not, after all, a disease!

As the majority of married couples want to practice periodic abstinence without medical assistance, we have been at pains to explain the method as simply and clearly as possible. We can assure our readers of generally excellent results when the method is self-applied, provided that the instructions have been strictly obeyed.

Whenever there are difficulties or uncertainties, however, a woman should consult her doctor and show him her menstrual calendar, which, needless to say, must be accurately and carefully kept.

2. Repetition of the most important rules

We give a summary of those rules whose observance is important and whose neglect has already been responsible for many failures.

1. Before the method is applied, it is essential to *know the exact cycle pattern*, that is to say, to have observed the cycles over a period of one year at least, and to continue to observe them accurately (Chapters III, §2, and IV).

2. A woman must know whether she is susceptible to *disturbances* of her cycle and what causes the disturbance (Chapters III, §3, and IV, §2).

3. *Triple* and *quadruple* cycle patterns should be calculated as quintuple patterns (Chapter VI, §3 b and §4 b).

4. Every woman should try to observe her *ovulation symptoms* and record her *temperature curve* (Chapters II, §2 and IV, §4) or make a glucose test (Chapter IV, §5).

5. In every case the woman shall keep regularly and methodically her *menstrual calendar* (Chapter IV, §3) and show it to her doctor at each consultation (Chapter IV).

6. *Caution* must be exercised in the *initial* application of the method (Chapter VI, §4 a, b).

7. Should a *disturbance* occur, the abstinence days must be increased. When this disturbance takes place before or during the ovulation period, abstinence must be maintained *until the next menstruation* (Chapter VI, §4 d).

8. *After childbirth*, extra caution is essential (Chapter VII, §1).

9. *After a birth or a miscarriage*, the cycle pattern is often different from what it was before; the same applies after serious illness (Chapters III, §3 d and VII, §1, §2, §3).

10. During the *first months of marriage* there sometimes occurs a change in the cycle pattern (Chapter VI, §4 a, b).

11. A *change in the way of life*—change of climate, change of diet, undereating (reducing diet), etc.—can equally produce a change in the cycle pattern (Chapters IV, §2 and VII, §6).

12. Anyone using contraceptives during the fertile days need not be surprised if an unexpected pregnancy occurs, because such methods are not secure and cause disturbances in the cycles.

13. Women who must, on doctor's orders, take *hormone* preparations (especially preparations from pituitary, follicle, or *corpus luteum* secretions or thyroids), can apply the method only with the greatest caution during this time and for a few months afterward, for these preparations can cause big disturbances in the cycle pattern (Chapters IV, §2 and VII, §6).

14. The cycle pattern alters in the course of life (Chapters III, §4, §5 and VI, §4 e). For this reason, it must be continually noted.

15. When the cycle pattern deviates considerably from the cycle pattern of 28 days (very short or very long cycles), its

tendency to veer toward the 28-day pattern must be taken into account (Chapter III, §4).

16. Ready-reckoners, simple formulae, tables, or menstrual calendars are not of themselves sufficient to ensure complete security. A woman must have an exact knowledge of her personal peculiarities and take careful note of any changes in her mode of life (Chapters IV and VI, §2).

17. When ovulation symptoms are observed (Chapter II, §2), *three* days are added to the abstinence days (Chapter VI, §4 c).

18. Observation of the temperature on waking and the glucose test are *insufficient* for marking off the sterile days at the start of the cycle (Chapter VI, §4 c).

Before they make public their experiences with the method, doctors must make certain that the married couples have fully adhered to these points, otherwise the report of their findings will be worthless.

IX

THE PRACTICAL RESULTS ACHIEVED BY THE NATURAL METHOD OF AVOIDING CONCEPTION

Has the method of periodic continence proved practical? That is a question many readers will ask. For this reason we give the following summary of the reports of doctors who have so far had practical experience with the method.

As early as 1915, Siegel gave an account in a German medical weekly[1] of the precise notes which had been made by his former teacher, Professor Wöhler (Freiburg), regarding 160 women who had become pregnant during the first five weeks of marriage. Sixty-five of these women had been married in the last week before menstruation and in all cases, without exception, menstruation occurred once more, a proof that conception is impossible during the last week of the cycle.

Professor Raoul de Guchteneere, the Belgian gynecologist and director of the Brussels Maternity Hospital, recognized at this early stage the significance of this incontestable experimental proof of the total sterility of the last days in a woman's cycle and, because of this—long before Ogino's works were published—advised those patients for whom pregnancy appeared inadvisable, to have sexual intercourse only during the last six days of the cycle. As De Guchteneere reported many times in 1931, pregnancy did not occur in any one of these

[1] *Deutsche med. Wochenschr.*

113

cases. When De Guchteneere became acquainted with Ogino's writings, he advised his patients to utilize the last 11 days of the cycle. Later, after Smulders had made public his findings, De Guchteneere also allowed the first days of the cycle to be utilized, and in all cases with success.

De Guchteneere reported in 1933[2] that observations which he had made of nine newly married couples completely agreed with Wöhler's findings. Dr. Remmelts, professor of gynecology in Batavia, Netherlands East Indies, gave an account of fourteen such cases in 1932,[3] and Ogino[4] of 56 such cases, all of which, without exception, testify to the sterility of women during the last days of the cycle.

De Guchteneere described (1933) the rare case where a woman of the working class, without the least technical training, had for years practiced planned birth control through periodic abstinence and postponement of sexual relations to the last 11 days. She claimed to have learned this secret from her mother, who had discovered it from her own observations made in the course of her marriage. This woman deliberately became pregnant on five occasions simply by changing the time of sexual intercourse to the period before the last 11 days.

Drs. R. L. Dickinson[5] and Bouwdijk-Bastieense[6] also reported quite unusual cases where simple, untrained women had successfully practiced birth control by taking advantage of a natural law whose existence scientific circles solidly contested at the time, and which many refuse to admit even today.

On account of its individual duration (according to the cycle lengths), a woman's sterility during the first days of the cycle was difficult to determine. Added to this was the formerly widely spread erroneous belief that a woman was most fertile at the time of menstruation, and least fertile in the middle of

[2] Revue franç. de gynéc. obst.
[3] Geneesk. Tijdschrift v. Nederl. Indie.
[4] Zentralblatt für Gynäkologie.
[5] American Journal of Obstetrics and Gynecology, 1927.
[6] Nederl. Tijdschrift v. Verl., 1932.

the cycle. Smulders refers to two cases in which this error led to a result contrary to the one desired. In one of these cases, a couple burdened with the care of many children, wished to avoid having more. Following the advice of a doctor to have intercourse only in the middle of the cycle, it was found that each time a pregnancy followed.

In the second case, a woman who wished to have children, and also following a doctor's advice, had intercourse on the days just preceding the cycle and for nine years remained childless. In both cases Dr. Smulders was able to advise these couples and the desired results were obtained. Dr. Knaus also refers to similar cases.[7]

The Spanish gynecologist and professor at Oviedo University, Dr. Macías de Torres, made a special study of the sterility of women during the first days of the cycle and assembled a series of practical experiences which likewise corroborate Knaus.[8]

Dr. J. G. H. Holt, the Dutch gynecologist, also made a detailed study of the sterile days at the start of the cycle, taking into consideration only dates marked by the women at the time on a special calendar, and excluding data supplied from memory. This study treats exclusively of couples who had already had children and who had, therefore, proved procreative. The results are given in Fig. 39.

That great work of Professor Hermann Knaus, *Die Physiologie der Zeugung des Menschen* (Vienna, 1953), furnishes a wealth of data assembled by him over the years from the cases he had observed. We have taken only one example from it (Fig. 40). In this book Knaus also provides a detailed description of the practical results which other doctors have achieved by his method (see Fig. 41).

In Japan, as early as 1923, Dr. Kyusaku Ogino published in part his theory and his practical experiences, which were not published in Europe until 1930 and 1932.[9] He had observed

---

[7] *Munch. Med. W.*, 1930.
[8] *Revue franç. de gynéc. obst.*, June, 1933.
[9] *Zentralblatt für Gynäkologie.*

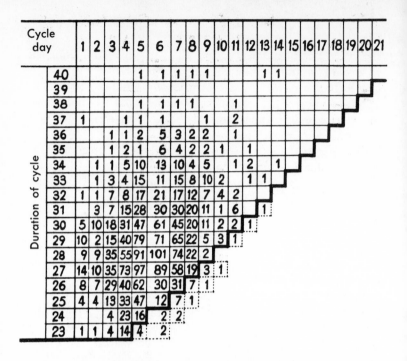

Cycle day	1	2	3	4	5	6	7	8	9	10	11	12	13	14	15	16	17	18	19	20	21
40				1		1	1	1	1				1	1							
39																					
38				1		1	1	1			1										
37	1			1	1	1			1		2										
36			1	1	2	5	3	2	2		1										
35			1	2	1	6	4	2	2	1		1									
34		1	1	5	10	13	10	4	5		1	2		1							
33		1	3	4	15	11	15	8	10	2		1	1								
32	1	1	7	8	17	21	17	12	7	4	2										
31		3	7	15	28	30	30	20	11	1	6		1								
30	5	10	18	31	47	61	45	20	11	2	2	1									
29	10	2	15	40	79	71	65	22	5	3	1										
28	9	9	35	55	91	101	74	22	2												
27	14	10	35	73	97	89	58	19	3	1											
26	8	7	29	40	62	30	31	7	1												
25	4	4	13	33	47	12	7	1													
24			4	23	16	2	2														
23	1	1	4	14	4	2															

(row label at left: Duration of cycle)

Fig. 39. Holt's table of 2,201 cohabitations, during the first part of the cycle, not one of which resulted in pregnancy (according to Smulders, 1952)

numerous couples over a period of years and reported, for example, upon a case which he had under observation for six years.

Dr. J. N. Smulders, who had advised well over a thousand couples in the course of the years, accumulated an exceedingly large amount of practical data. In his book, published in Dutch in 1934, he devotes more than a hundred pages to reports on individual cases. Most of these he had personally followed for over three years, and in every case successful results had been obtained. After his premature death in 1939, Manz Verlag, Munich, drew upon the papers containing his observations to publish in 1952 a new edition of his book, *Periodische Enthaltung in der Ehe*, containing a wealth of most valuable data.

Dr. Holt, mentioned above and the close collaborator of

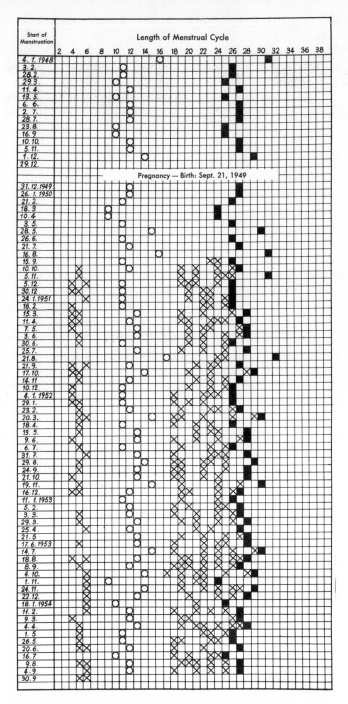

Fig. 40. Table showing start and length of cycle, date of ovulation, and of sexual intercourse. Under the column, "Start of Menstruation," the *day* of the month is given first, followed by the *month*

Smulders, testified many times to the veritable mountain of letters of gratitude received by Dr. Smulders from those who had used his method with complete success.[10]

Dr. Holt says in his book, *Marriage and Periodic Continence: The Natural Method of Scientific Family Regulation*,[11] that they were both convinced that success was certain in all cases where the method was correctly applied. It can often, he says, be adopted in cases of serious chronic illness, but only under the supervision of a doctor.[12]

In March, 1937, Dr. Leo J. Latz, professor of gynecology at Loyola University, Chicago, published in the *Illinois Medical Journal*, in collaboration with Dr. E. Reiner, his co-worker, an account of their numerous observations. He stated that in the autumn of 1932 they began advising their patients to practice abstinence during the fertile days as a means of avoiding conception. They had corresponded with more than 25,000 women, and, up to the time of writing, they had received only 59 complaints of failures. The writer then proceeds to show, with the help of dates, how nearly all these failures had been due either to mistakes or to negligences in the application of the method. He claims that at least 57 out of the 59 cases could not be attributed to a deficiency in the method. Indeed, the few complaints which they had received from married couples constituted such an extraordinarily small percentage that they held themselves justified in considering that, for normal, healthy women with regular menstruation, the natural method of avoiding conception could be regarded as trustworthy. Their experiences to date were another proof that the method for the avoidance of conception the natural way, according to Knaus-Ogino, was "practical, usable, and reliable."

[10] Cf. *Artsenblad*, Amsterdam, 1933.
[11] Rev. English ed., London and New York: Longmans, Green & Co., 1960.
[12] The publishing house of Franz Deuticke, Vienna, issued in the summer of 1959 a remarkable work by Dr. Holt, *Geburtenregelung auf biologischem Wege*, which contains observations made over ten years and deals especially with the relationship between fertility and the temperature of the female body. It can be recommended to doctors and informed lay people.

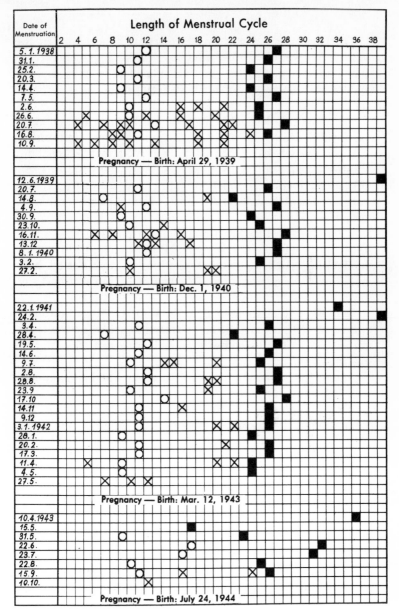

Fig. 41. Self-observations made by Dr. J. M. (lady practitioner), London (according to Knaus). Under the column, "Date of Menstruation," the *day* of the month is given first, followed by the *month*

Dr. Latz later published other practical observations in the *American Journal of Obstetrics and Gynecology* (Jan., 1942) and a book on the rhythm method. Figure 42 is an example of one of his tabular compilations. It deals, in this instance, with 11,222 cases.

We must call particular attention to the book by that most distinguished Swiss specialist, Dr. Anton Stecher, *Zeitwahl in der Ehe*, which has appeared in many editions. It contains numerous practical observations, all testifying to the accuracy of the method. Especially interesting and instructive is one case, documented with precise dates, which the author observed over a period of 17 years.

A number of other Swiss and German practitioners—among them Drs. Frühauf, G. K. Döring, H. J. Gerstner, E. Frey, Gerhard Ockel, Riebold, Labhart, Guthmann, and Vetter—have published articles and books showing the trustworthiness of the Knaus method.

It is interesting to note that Professor C. Ruge, a former opponent of the Knaus theory, changed his views as the result of his own critical investigations and became a supporter of the theory.[13]

Among the British supporters of Knaus are the London physician J. Young, in the *British Medical Journal* (May, 1936), and of Dr. G. Pugh Smith of Cardiff, who reported (1941) in the same review a case observed by him for a period of four years. We also mention the interesting observation data made by Dr. J. A. Pryde, an English practitioner, and published in the *British Medical Journal*, also in 1941.

In 1947 a book, *Na prahu manželstvi*, in favor of the Knaus method could still be published in Czechoslovakia. The author, Dr. Josef Navrátil, asserted that doctors made a mistake to fight the method solely on the basis that it appeared to them to be "too Catholic."

Voices in favor of the Knaus method have also been raised in the Soviet Union, namely those of A. Schepetinskaja (1935)

[13] *Zentralblatt für Gynäkologie*, 1943.

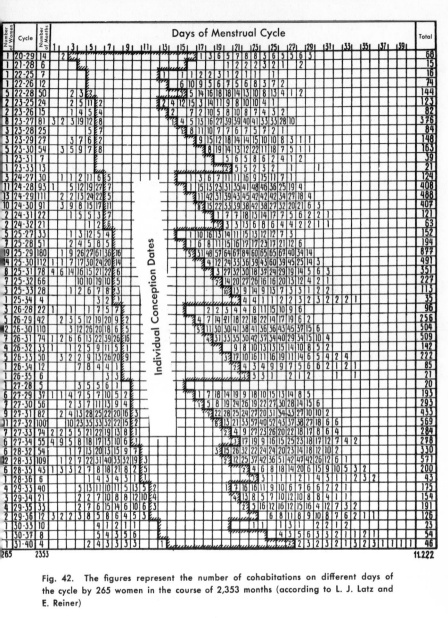

Fig. 42. The figures represent the number of cohabitations on different days of the cycle by 265 women in the course of 2,353 months (according to L. J. Latz and E. Reiner)

and A. Jarzew (1938). The Danish practitioner, Dr. H. Leun-bach, as also the Dutch doctor Engelhard, of the gynecological clinic of Gröningen, have professed their faith in Knaus.

In the Spanish edition of Dr. Eric Knight's book *Matrimonios, Hijos, Dios* (Barcelona, 1955), the Spanish editor, Dr. G. Nieto, writes (p. 181): "During the last 17 years, in the innumerable cases in which I have recommended . . . the method . . . I have not known of more than three cases of pregnancy. But in these I am certain that the women, consciously or unconsciously, made a mistake in the counting of the cycle days *in order to conceive* the child which they, if not their husbands, desired. I must suffer as a scapegoat for these women."

The South American specialist F. Carvalho Azevado made a careful examination of the question of periodic sterility and described [14] 50 cases he had followed for a period of three and a half years. Not only did he defend the Knaus theory against attack but he came to the conclusion that numerous physical and organic disturbances caused by unnatural contraceptive practices would disappear when the couples used the Knaus method which follows the laws of nature. He also saw in this method the best means for combating abortion.

Another South American study of the subject was made by Dr. Wolffenbuttel and published in the Portuguese language in Puerto Alegre, Brazil.

Dr. Armando Zabala Sáenz of Buenos Aires, published in 1934, with the ecclesiastical *non obstat*, a book on the Knaus-Ogino method entitled *El Problema de los Hijos*. In this he concluded: "All observations we have made enable us to affirm categorically that the method of periodic continence offers full security on the condition that account is taken of the individual variations that may occur in the cycles."

The noted embryologist, Dr. C. G. Hartman, of the Carnegie Institute at Washington, in *Birth Control Review* (May, 1933) stated his conviction that when the Knaus-Ogino method was followed exactly it offered more security than could be ob-

[14] *Ann. Brasil. Gynec.* I (1936), pp. 255, 283, 386–405, 474–511.

tained by any other means suggested by American marriage counseling services.

The Miller Clinic at Hobart (Geneva, N.Y.) published [15] interesting data concerning 97 couples of which the women had 12 varying forms of cycles and were of 8 different nationalities. These observations confirmed, without a single exception, the exactness of the Knaus method. Among them was a case in which the sterile days had been utilized for a period of 11 years and the marriage had remained childless. A simple deviation of the days used in the twelfth year led to a pregnancy. In July, 1933, Dr. Miller wrote the author he had prepared his article a year before, and that it was based on observation of 1,429 cases over a period of years. In January, 1935, Miller published further data he had collected in the review, *Clinical Medicine and Surgery.*

The Journal of the American Medical Association (Feb. 10, 1934) confirmed the scientific exactness of the method and called attention to its spiritual, moral and social advantages. The same is true of the medical review *Clinical Medicine and Surgery* (Waukegan, Illinois, 1934) and the medical periodical *Mutual Professional News* (New York, May, 1934).

More recently in the United States, books have appeared in support of the method. Among these are: *Marriage: A Medical and Sacramental Study* (1955) by John Ryan, M.D., and Alan Keenan, O.F.M., and *Family Limitation* (rev. ed. 1961) by John Ryan, M.D., both published by Sheed and Ward, New York.

The Rhythm Way to Family Happiness by John P. Murphy, M.D., and John D. Laux, M.D. (New York, Hawthorn Books, rev. ed. 1960) contains a number of very precise charts compiled from the observations of American physicians.

Marriage and the Family by Dr. Alphonse H. Clemens, Director of the Marriage Counselling Center, Catholic University of America (Englewood, N.J., Prentice-Hall), also supports the method.

Another American work, now translated into various lan-

[15] *Surg. Gyn. Obst.*, June, 1933.

guages, is *Natural Birth Control without Contraceptives* by Professor John A. O'Brien (Huntingdon, Indiana) which confirms the good results obtained in the United States through use of the method.

The enumeration of reports of practical experiences which support the method could be very much extended. We shall, however, content ourselves with repeating a statement made as early as 1933 by Dr. Raoul de Guchteneere (*Saint Luc Médical, No. 2*): "A small number of well observed clinical cases, such as Smulders reports, proves more and refutes objections better than the most learned dissertations."

The method for determining the sterile days which we have described stands on a solid foundation. Provided that it is correctly put to use, it surpasses in practical security all unnatural contraceptive practices.

PART THREE

MARRIAGE, FAMILY, AND BIRTH CONTROL

X

THE SEXUAL INSTINCT

Of all the physiological instincts, none affects human life and civilization so strongly as the sexual one. It is connected with nature's highest purpose. The procreation of new life is an act of such magnitude and power that everything associated with it must necessarily have a potent and profound repercussion upon a human being. Hence the spiritual exaltation and happiness which accompany the ordered and normal manifestation of this instinct.

Nature is so ordered that no individual living creature can be generated independently of the life preceding it. New life can spring only from life already in existence. A new human being demands that there be first a father and a mother. The procreative faculty, which the Creator has planted in every human being, is a gift of tremendous importance, for it makes it possible to pass on to posterity the life handed down through the medium of long generations.

Since there is in nature no other way of creating new generations to replace us, procreation is one of the greatest and most responsible tasks which the human race has to perform upon this earth, and for the performance of which it must render an account to the Author of life.

Anyone who has once understood the sexual life in its full significance could thereafter think and speak of it only in a spirit of respect and awe. He will realize the baseness and stupidity of making the sexual process, and everything connected with it, the sole and most important source, so to speak, of sophisticated witticisms and coarse stories. This sacred mystery is distorted and ridiculed in the amusement page of many magazines, in novels and films, in the theater, as well as in a great deal of commercial advertising which exploits it.

He will understand, too, just why the exercise of this faculty has been regulated by all peoples in all ages by sacred laws and surrounded with significant rites, and why Jesus Christ elevated marriage, the sole state for the legitimate exercise of the sexual power, to the dignity of a sacrament.

The human being experiences instincts as powerful natural forces demanding expression, and the strongest of these is the sexual instinct. It would be inaccurate to say that this instinct is an urge toward procreation, for, considered on its own, its urge is merely toward its fulfillment, that is to say, toward sexual union, and it displays itself in its full strength even when natural reasons render procreation impossible. A conscious urge toward procreation is not inherent in the instinct itself, and it is only as the result of experience and reflection that we recognize the primary end assigned by nature to the instinct, namely, the *conservation of the species and the propagation of the human race*, which could not be ensured without the sexual instinct.

The exercise of the sexual instinct cannot be left to the arbitrary whim of the individual. In the animal kingdom the sexual faculty is instinctively regulated and makes itself known only at certain periods (rut). Among humans, however, *the instinct must be directed by reason*. Man recognizes the purpose of the instinct, and the consequences of its exercise and is responsible, therefore, for this as he is for all his actions. Since the instinct, of its very nature, urges toward union with a person of the other sex, and since a new life can be called into being only by the normal gift of self, all abnormal exercise of the instinct is contrary to nature, an abuse of the creative power, and, hence, a grave wrong.

The natural satisfaction of the sexual instinct transcends the moment and the individual person, for in any event there is involved in it another person, the partner in the act, another human being whom we may never use merely as a thing for the serving of a personal end. It can never be permissible to look upon a human creature as no more than an instrument for the satisfaction of a passing pleasure. When they are associated as sex partners, a man and a woman are individuals of *equal value and equal rights*. That is why their relationships must be ordered, subject to reason, and in accord with human dignity.

The sexual act has the most profound repercussions upon the spiritual life of both partners. To all pure-minded people, who are not the victims of a false mental outlook, sexual surrender is an experience of the greatest spiritual profundity. In the sexual surrender, there is the deepest awareness that it is an abandonment of the whole person to another, the revealing of oneself to another in a very special way, the offering of the very heart of one's innermost being. If in this surrender one of the partners feels that he or she has been misused or betrayed by the other, it gives rise to the greatest pain and humiliation— one has given oneself to someone who was unworthy. For those whose senses have not become blunted by outside influences or by their own mode of life, sexual surrender is, therefore, a most profound and moving experience which leaves behind it a lasting impression in the soul, spiritually joining together both partners in mysterious fashion, and creating a type of spiritual relationship. Even when the two people concerned are no longer in personal contact, they still retain the feeling of a certain spiritual affinity with the one to whom sexual surrender was made.

Sexual intercourse is so intimate and lasting an experience that those who have remained pure in this domain can make this surrender only if they are certain that their deepest feelings will not be wounded or betrayed, and if they have the desire to remain permanently united with the other person. For sexual union implies a total and personal surrender to one another for life.

It must be freely admitted that the delicacy of feeling for the sublimity of the sexual life can be lost, and that with many people, as a result of faulty education, it never fully develops.

From the physiological point of view, sexual intercourse is not just a means to the procreation of new life, although this is its primary task. For often, indeed in the majority of cases, procreation is not possible on purely natural grounds. Even if married couples let nature take its own course and do nothing to limit the number of their children, the number of procreations would stand in great disparity to the number of sexual acts. When, furthermore, one knows that a woman is not fertile every day of her life, that even in her best years the sterile days are incomparably more numerous than the fertile days, it will be realized that procreation is not the only purpose which nature has intended for sexual intercourse. As sexual desire exists independently of capability for fertilization, nature herself has taken care that the sexual act will serve some other natural design, apart from procreation.

Sexual union constitutes an event of some consequence for the human body. As a result of it, certain substances pass from the man's body into that of the woman and become transformed and assimilated by the female organism. As nature has so arranged it that the sterile days should far outnumber the fertile days, it seems that much importance has been placed on the transfer of these substances which have a beneficial influence on the physiological processes of the woman.

From the sexual act, accordingly, there springs *in a certain sense* a physical relationship between man and woman and, hence, in the surrender there exists something irrevocable. The beneficial influence of the sexual act upon a woman's health can be judged by observation of women who have got married late in life and who become rejuvenated with dramatic suddenness and, as it were, bloom again. Upon the physiological functions of the male organism, normal sexual relations also exert a beneficial and healthy influence and in a special way the man's nature responds and adapts itself to that of his wife.

Viewed in this light, the need for prenuptial chastity and

marital fidelity acquires a profound meaning. It is a question of the actual chaste bearing of the body. The term is not used comparatively, nor is it to be understood in a figurative but in a literal sense. Nature herself demands prenuptial chastity and permanent monogamy. For the chaste bearing of our body, we are accountable to our marriage partner.

As the source of a new life, the importance of sexual intercourse transcends both spouses. Even if every individual sexual act does not lead to conception, procreation nevertheless continues to be the primary design of nature and of the Creator, and, from the point of view of humanity as a whole, appears the general and permanent consequence of the sexual life. This aspect, therefore, has far-reaching social implications; it is the spring of life from which human society renews itself. For that reason, man is also accountable to society for his behavior, which must be so conducted as to take into due consideration the needs of the individual and those of the community.

The pleasure which sexual activity affords is of its nature one of the most important sources of joy for mankind. Although the pleasure attendant on orderly sexual relations is good in itself, nevertheless in this very source of pleasure there is a danger to the moral equilibrium of man. Because of the strength of the instinct, man is all too easily inclined to strive after the pleasures of sexuality even when there are serious obligations opposed to so doing, and to seek satisfaction of the instinct in an unnatural way if the natural consequences of the sexual act must be avoided. The sexual instinct, more easily than any of the other instincts, gains in dominion over a man and enslaves his spirit.

Man as a being with body and soul is so constituted that intellect and free will should direct the instincts. The submission of the instincts to the guidance of reason and will is what constitutes the dignity of man. When passion gains such control that the will no longer follows the clear judgment of reason but, instead, abandons itself to the demands of the instinct, then there is a degradation of man and an abandonment of human dignity. He no longer does what he knows to be right, but rather what his carnal desires urge him to do; leadership by the spirit has been lost; man has ceased to be the complete man. The body, which should be the docile servant of the spirit, has become its master.

This inversion of the natural order affects a man's whole life, and according to the degree to which his spirit has become enslaved by his bodily desires, will he be debased. He can sink to the level of a worthless sensualist, with no higher interests in life than satisfaction of desire. The larger the number of sensualists in a community, the more they gain ground among the leading classes of a people, the more fatal the consequences for the whole of its social life.

The attitude toward sex is not, therefore, simply a personal matter—it is a very far-reaching social matter also. It is not right to promote sexual license for youth, for it is of the utmost importance to the community that the rising generation should learn self-discipline and not evade responsibility and sacrifice. One of the most important tasks of education is to make man the master of his psychological instincts. The ideal of the moral personality is the person who gives his instincts play according to the laws of nature and of the Creator. By this we are not preaching flight from the world. Renunciation is not an end in itself and should not be sought for itself. It is only good in so far as the motives that inspire it are reasonable. Mastery over instinct is not the equivalent of abstinence. It merely implies the subordination of instinct to the guidance of reason which, in many circumstances of life can, it is true, amount to the same thing as abstinence.

The instincts are a gift of the Creator and consequently good in themselves. The moral ideal toward which we must strive is not, therefore, to free ourselves of desire, but to preserve the freedom of our will in spite of it.

XI

MARRIAGE AND THE FAMILY

1. Mutual relations of the sexes

When a man and a woman form a union, each represents his or her entire sex to the other. Their union is not only a private and personal affair, but in every individual case it is also an impersonal and timeless meeting of the sexes. Every community of man with woman is a manifestation of the great community of the entire masculine sex with the entire feminine sex.

The attempt has been made to represent marriage as a mixture of friendship and sexual sensuality, but such a conception fails to see the essence of marriage. Conjugal love between man and woman is basically different from friendship. Whereas the latter does not of its nature tend to fix its attention upon one of the opposite sex, is not confined to a single person but can easily embrace a whole group, conjugal love is exclusively directed to one particular person of the opposite sex.

Friends do not necessarily pursue the same aims as those they hold in friendship, whereas conjugal love is fixed directly on the person of the opposite sex and includes this person, body and soul, in its present plans and those for the future.

The love of man and woman is not an illusion of the sexes, but a consequence of their nature, their difference, and their capacity for completion. Man and woman are indeed equal but

133

in nature different. The difference affects not only the outward bodily form but extends to the last cell. Allied to this fundamental physical difference, there is an equally wide difference in the psychological make-up.

The complementary action of the sexes upon each other is not merely of a general and nonselective nature. Everyone has a personality of his own with special talents and special physical and psychological qualities. Partly as a result of heredity and partly as a result of environment, he is different from all other men, a particular "ego." Hence everyone feels the need for personal completion—suitable for oneself—through the opposite sex. Every man seeks "his" woman, and every woman "her" man. The ties of sexual love are deeply rooted in human nature, and, therefore, the revelation of love is a powerful experience.

It is very regrettable that the nature of conjugal love and its creative power are so often misunderstood and actually replaced by a mixture of friendship and sensuality such as in the so-called "companionate marriages." Love is thereby robbed of its essential characteristics, permanence, and unity. Friends can be changed, and sensuality nearly always finds satisfaction in relations with persons of the opposite sex, but that is not love. Those who ask no more than this from life remain oblivious to the essence of sexual love and deprive themselves of an important and pure source of happiness and of strong forces and impulses which contribute to the development and perfection of their personality.

Since both lovers differ from one another, but are drawn to one another by their need for completion, there develops between them a tension which they know to be creative. Every true love is creative, and sexual love is not only creative physically but spiritually.

Through the mutual trust, the idealization of the sexes in love, and the desire really to become what the other is seeking, many dormant forces are aroused in young people and brought into play. The lovers unite in the great work of educating and perfecting themselves and one another; through the action of each upon the other, they become spiritually richer and deeper personalities. This "mobilization of forces" could hardly be replaced by any other educational method. Society would suffer great harm if this source of strength ran dry because of the general introduction of "free love," of unrestrained sexual license.

The affectionate union with another person brings sunshine into the heart and proves extremely valuable in many circumstances of life. In sorrow, especially, there are considerable consolation and support in knowing that one is not alone. The consciousness of having someone who lives for us, and for whom we live, is often a source of strength and a deterrent from thoughtless actions.

Life together in marriage is influenced by many factors—by the qualities, the character, and the past life of the partner, by the right choice of spouse, by the conditions under which the marriage was contracted and which will sustain it in any crisis that may arise.

The first encounter of an adolescent with sex makes a deep impression. The final pattern of behavior adopted toward the sexual impulses during the formative years can exercise a lasting influence on his character and on his nature.

The more the value of the indissoluble marital union is appreciated and treasured, so much the less effort of will does it cost to remain pure. The more the adolescent succeeds in concentrating all his forces on being the first and only one to that other person—as yet unknown—who will bring him the lasting completion which his nature requires, the easier it becomes for him to remain true, in advance, to that person. Likewise, as reasonably early marriages are natural and healthy, premarital abstinence constitutes for both sexes the ideal preparation for marriage. It is not only the training of the will but even more the recognition of moral values and the cultivation of a sense of responsibility which constitute the foundations of character formation and consequently the most important aspects of education.

The more young people are impressed by the realization that

marriage is not a playground for sexual energy, but a vocation, the fulfillment of an important task in life, and that the ultimate means of marriage (in the natural order) lies in irrevocable mutual surrender, not in the satisfaction of the flesh, so the more worthwhile will appear the "saving of oneself" for the life companion. When all sexual energy is concentrated on one person in marriage and when there is nothing before it with which to make a comparison, the unwavering fidelity, which is the foundation of every union, is already largely assured.

2. Sexual intercourse

Sexual intercourse is an integral part of conjugal love. It is not just something externally incidental to the task of procreation, but the most intimate and profound expression of the total surrender inspired by love. Through love, the sexual surrender is enriched and protected from the danger of sensual brutality and insatiable lust; the manifestation of desire becomes controlled and orderly. In the words of Father Max Pribilla:

> Conjugal love is very different from the mere desire for physical union and sensual pleasure. It is a "twosome" which in the middle of a cold, hard world affords a sense of warmth and security and which sees in physical union the expression and symbol of the spiritual love, surrender, trust and fidelity which it is seeking. In this way a strong natural instinct is satisfied and tamed at the same time and becomes an instrument not of destruction but of construction.[1]

Love and sexual intercourse are not exclusively a means to the accomplishment of procreation; they have another purpose also which concerns the married pair. As many false prejudices on the moral value of sexual relations in marriage are prevalent, we would like to stress that the normal surrender of husband and wife has nothing in it inferior, "animal-like," or undigni-

[1] Max Pribilla in the German Catholic review, *Stimmen der Zeit* (October, 1931), p. 25.

fied, but that it is an act which is morally good. This also applies unreservedly to elderly married couples, provided that health or some serious reason does not demand considerate restraint by one of the spouses.

To renounce sexual intercourse in marriage is not in itself a more perfect thing to do. Only if the renunciation arises from higher motives is there greater moral perfection in it. In the natural order, sexual intercourse in marriage, since it corresponds more closely to the nature of marriage, is morally more perfect than is abstinence. In certain circumstances, abstinence may be nothing short of a violation of duty and can make conjugal fidelity very difficult for the other partner.

For the married couple, the sexual life is of physiological and psychological significance. We mentioned earlier that the "becoming one flesh" produces a physical and psychological affinity between the couple which effects a mutual adjustment in the course of sexual experience. Through sexual intercourse, the spiritual union is preserved and deepened and mutual love is strengthened. Furthermore, sexual relaxation gives to the married couple refreshment and pleasure, something which is of no little importance in the hard struggle for existence. For this reason married people should not, without a weighty reason, reduce or abandon sexual relations.

Sexual desire, which springs from sincere love and is the expression of the conjugal union, can and should be responded to intimately by the couple. This applies to a young wife in particular, for if she underestimates or, even worse, despises the sexual aspect, she is in danger of disrupting the harmony of the marriage and encouraging her husband to be unfaithful.

There is a tendency today to make a real cult out of the sensual aspect of sex, and harm has been done by the circulation of books which "explain the technique of sexual relations." We most emphatically warn engaged and married couples not to study such literature which, far from helping to foster married life, can only serve to destroy it. A husband and wife who are in love will experience the purest joy in their surrender if they allow nature and their love to guide them.

Since man is endowed with reason and moral sense, to isolate sensuality to a sphere of its own is always to lower his status. To sensuality belongs a subordinate role; it should only be aroused and savored in the service of love, and in harmony with the requirements of nature.

In connection with the complete surrender of love, a couple will not want to refrain nevertheless from the display of all kinds of intimate caresses. It is right that it should be so, for if the surrender of self is the expression of mutual love, and if it grows, as it were, out of these other signs of affection, then it is very probable that the carnal act will take place normally and completely and that both partners will achieve a natural measure of satisfaction, which is very important to their sexual life together in marriage. Generally then, no "technique" is needed.

It must be clearly stressed that sexual intercourse should not be an egotistical act on the part of one of the partners; the wishes of each of the two must outweigh the satisfaction of individual needs. If love is really present on both sides, one will not remain indifferent to the importance of seeing that the other partner in sexual intercourse has in fact also got from it the full measure of pleasure that nature intended. The obligation to show such consideration rests primarily on the husband, for very often the sexual sensation develops more slowly in a woman and continues longer than in a man.

For this reason, present-day doctors strongly recommend that sexual intercourse should not begin and end abruptly but that it be framed with a prelude and epilogue of affectionate and intimate caresses, so that the wife too may enjoy the satisfaction which nature intended her to have. As a result of being constantly unsatisfied by sexual intercourse, a woman's nervous system is adversely affected, and she suffers physically and psychologically. Furthermore, she is deprived of a pleasure to which nature gave her the same rights as the man. Nobody should treat these matters with indifference. A woman can become sexually cold and frigid when she is shown no consideration or understanding—not even good will—by her husband, and when she feels that, in his selfish egoism, he thinks only of himself and the satisfaction of his own desire. In this way the woman is not only unjustly deprived of a part of the joys of life but the harmony of the marriage also suffers, as then the husband generally finds no further pleasure in living with his wife. Hence it can never be sufficiently emphasized that the conjugal act, far from being egotistical, is an act of mutual love.

If a couple, in spite of good will, cannot achieve unison in their sexual relations, or if there are other hindrances or physiological difficulties, they should not be shy about consulting a doctor.

As the first sexual experience is of decisive significance for the subsequent sexual life of the couple, it is essential that the first sexual advance should be made with great care so that the delicate feelings of the woman will not be upset. As pain, mostly slight but which can also be severe, is attendant upon the woman's first experience of sexual intercourse, the man must show consideration and restraint.

Satisfaction and pleasure from sexual intercourse come only gradually to a woman. On that account it would be unreasonable and selfish on the part of the husband to expect from his wife, during the first days and weeks of their marriage, responses for which she is not yet ready. By doing so, he could easily disgust her, and the first weeks of marriage, instead of giving pleasure, could provide only disappointment.

A husband should have understanding for the modesty and the many inhibitions which the young wife brings to the marriage. If nothing is done by force, but with patience and affection, the two will become adjusted to the new state of life. This mutual self-adjustment is not easy and does not take place all at once.

The duty of the first weeks of marriage is the sexual integration of two people, reared in different circumstances and endowed with different temperaments. It is a duty which, even in the face of difficulties, must be performed with patience and mutual understanding.

The monthly process which takes place in the female body is a rhythmical process which repeats itself within a certain space of time and which manifests itself not only in the regular recurrent bleeding but also influences the woman's general disposition. During the days of menstruation, a woman is not physically or psychologically as vigorous as usual; she is less able to do physical work and needs consideration. The husband should make allowance for her increased psychological sensitivity during this period and be correspondingly considerate to her.

On hygienic, as well as aesthetic grounds, sexual intercourse is inadvisable during menstruation.

Procreation should be regarded as the primary aim of every matrimonial union, and one should prepare consciously for a task so charged with responsibility. Formerly, preparation for the act of procreation was hardly possible, for it was erroneously believed that each act of sexual intercourse could result in conception; today, however, we know that, provided the couple are in good health, procreation can be controlled. Hence is the responsibility greater and the obligation for preparation more serious (see Chapter VI, §5).

Sexual intercourse can also be continued during pregnancy, with certain restrictions, but a wife will need more consideration as the date of the birth draws nearer. However, relations can usually be maintained up to the seventh month of pregnancy, though with greater consideration for the woman and regard for the child in her womb.

In some women, intercourse during the first three months of pregnancy can easily bring on a miscarriage. Hence it is advisable for women who are inclined to have miscarriages to practice abstinence during the first three and last three months of pregnancy.

The lying-in period naturally requires strict abstinence. It would be brutal on the part of a husband if he did not exercise control and sought intercourse at a time when his wife has been weakened by her confinement, and when, moreover, her genital organs are particularly vulnerable. Such a thoughtless action can end in disaster, because infection and laceration can easily occur during this period. Not until after the expiration of six weeks can intercourse be resumed; after a miscarriage, the woman must also be spared for some weeks.

During lactation, menstruation does not take place with many women for a long time, as a result of which some believe themselves incapable of conception. At the start of breast feeding, the capacity for conception is indeed slight, but it would be a mistake to believe that fertilization is impossible. After a while, the ovaries resume their activity and menstruation reappears, but if a fresh pregnancy has taken place before the reappearance of menstruation, naturally this will still not appear and the woman will imagine that the reason for this is lactation.

The occurrence of a fresh pregnancy, soon after childbirth, can greatly injure a woman's health. Because of this, it is advisable to allow the lapse of a year or two. We have already explained (Chapter VII, §1) how this is possible without practicing total abstinence or having recourse to contraceptive measures.

Marriage often goes through a period of crisis during the climacteric years of the woman. Her disposition will be affected by the physical changes which are taking place. After she has reached a certain age, a woman is released by nature from her obligation to serve humanity by childbearing. She can enter the last phase of her life free from the exhaustion of pregnancy and childbirth and the care of her children. Those to whom she has given birth are probably now grown up and already engaged in the battle of life, and, far from needing help any longer from their parents, they can be of assistance to them.

The time of the change of life varies. It generally begins around the age of 46. The change-over usually lasts for three years, but the period, too, varies with the individual. The ovaries and uterus gradually cease to perform their functions, menstruation is frequently absent, reappears, and finally disappears for good. Troublesome symptoms also appear—hot flushes, perspiration, depression, a general indisposition, etc.

Before and during the climacteric years, sexual desire in the woman usually increases, and she feels a correspondingly greater need for affection and tender caresses. The sexual instinct once again, one last time, demands satisfaction and gratification. In this tender embrace there comes to her the frightening question of whether the man, now that she is growing older, will continue to be a faithful and loving companion to her who had stood by him in faithful and loving devotion during the best and finest years of her life.

In nearly all large cities, medical marriage advisory centers have been set up. As advice can do much to relieve matrimonial distress and avert many a crisis, these centers as such are to be welcomed. Yet it must be borne in mind that marriage is only partly a physical affair and that a doctor is consequently not competent to deal with many matrimonial difficulties. The success of the advice given is still too dependent upon the personal beliefs of the consultant doctor. We object on principle to marriage advisory centers which are nothing more than signposts to contraceptive practices and abortion. Again, such advisory centers do not fulfill their purpose if they do not take cognizance of the new method of natural birth control and withhold from married couples full instruction upon the fertile and sterile days.

In the task of advising on marriage problems, such a center should have available, in addition to the doctor, a priest, a lawyer, and an experienced social worker.

3. The family

The lifelong union of man and woman should be for both a means to the development and expansion of the personality. Although in their marriage they have become integrated together in a unique way, the couple have not sunk their individual personalities in each other; without ceasing to be individuals they act as a unit. Through the mutual help and encouragement it affords, marriage can and should be a way to the acquisition of personalities richer than those they would probably have achieved if the couple had remained single.

This mutual, personal, and positively valuable help does not bind husband and wife together in one person but in a unity of a higher order, in a new social community which, because of its character and the extent of its obligation, differs radically from all other institutions. So great was the importance attached by the Creator to the realization of this closely knit community form, that He created man and woman different in the ways already mentioned so that together they might find completion.

This new unity, in which a couple travel the path to perfection together, in no way signifies a withdrawal from the rest of human society. On the contrary, no other union is so beneficial to humanity as the married one whose purpose transcends husband and wife; marriage is for human nature its source of renewal, conservation, and growth. Quite correctly may one describe the family as the primary cell of society.

The child is the natural fruit of conjugal love, and hence to the greatest extent the fulfillment of the natural meaning of marriage lies in propagation of the species. It is in parenthood that most people discover for the first time the depths of their being. Many reach full maturity of personality through parenthood which, on this account, must be recognized as one of the most important means to the realization of the individual personality. Hitherto latent and dormant powers and tendencies are revealed in the anxious care with which they surround their children and through the affection bred of mutual help and unselfish love.

It would be too much to expect of a husband and wife that they should not give themselves to one another except with the deliberate intention of procreation. Nature herself has so constituted the sexual act that in its manifestation the conscious faculties, reason and will, give way to a powerful spiritual impulse—love.

Moreover, sexual intercourse is not designed by nature merely for procreation. The deliberate intention to have, as well as the opposite intention not to have, children constitutes something of a disturbing element during the surrender itself.

Yet there must be readiness on the part of the married couple to welcome wholeheartedly into the bosom of the family the children who result from their affectionate union. This does not imply that the number of the children and the times of their births should not be regulated by the parents as the result of conscientious and reasoned reflection.

The child is an essential part of marriage because the primary object of this state is to beget descendants. Childless marriage should be the exception. Those who are blessed with health of mind and body and who can, therefore, expect to produce equally healthy descendants, should especially do everything possible to have as large a family as the health of the mother and their circumstances in life permit.

This is not to say that every wife should produce a large number of children. The task of marriage is not simply to conceive as many children as possible; there is the equally important one of rearing and educating them to be worthwhile citizens. The children should reach at least the same moral and intellectual standard as that of their parents and in keeping with their social level. Should this, generally speaking, not be recognized, then civilization would deteriorate and population increase would be deprived of one of its essential purposes—the preservation of civilization and its advancement to higher standards. Unnaturally large families form no part of the duties of the married state. The object is the normal family about which we shall speak more fully (Chapter XII, §2).

All healthy-minded men and women have a natural desire for offspring. It fills them with happiness to see their own individual characteristics, combined with those of their beloved partner, continuing on in the child. In spite of troubles and sacrifices, they devote themselves willingly to the training of these new beings who bear their characteristics, and they are happy if they can realize in the children that for which they themselves perhaps strove in vain. The desire for offspring can also be stimulated by outer circumstances, as, for example, the wish to be able to leave one's property to one's own children.

The bonds of matrimony are essentially strengthened by the

presence of children. The big and difficult task which the rearing and training of their children lays upon the parents gives the latter a common objective, a common round of duties, and tides them over the many difficulties which arise in the course of the marriage.

In normal circumstances, the education of the children, particularly during their early years, must be the duty of the parents. Generally speaking, nobody can perform this laborious and self-sacrificing task with such selflessness as they. From the point of view of the spiritual life of the child, also, the importance of growing up in the family circle is not to be underestimated. While we may feel the deepest gratitude and admiration for the unselfish work of members of religious orders, teachers, and nurses, we must admit nevertheless that despite their almost superhuman efforts they cannot take the place of parents.

We also consider that attention to the social and economic factors is indispensable to healthy development of family life. It is difficult to expect that an ideal family life could be led by people who live in material misery, without hope of any betterment of their wretched circumstances, whose minds are a prey to bitterness and despair, and who seek forgetfulness in alcohol.

4. The unity of marriage

So intimate and significant a union of the mind and body of a man and a woman as is marriage cannot be looked upon otherwise than as a union existing between two people only, a union which is enduring and indissoluble. Only those who fail to recognize the real nature of marriage could become parties to divorce and remarriage. We believe that the separation of a man and wife is contrary to the nature of sexual life and of love.

Moreover, from the social aspect, divorce is unnatural as the following consideration clearly shows: The conservation of the human race requires that every fertile married couple should produce an average of three to four children. The education of these children forms a tie between both parents until they are old. In the evening of life, when the children have grown up and are self-supporting, a desire for divorce is indeed unusual, for the long years together, especially in the prime of life, the shared sex life and common destiny, and, lastly, parenthood, have made husband and wife so accustomed and so adapted to one another that they would find separation a burden' in later life.

The bond which unites a man to a woman has been in existence since the dawn of human history and will endure until its end. Within it is held the fate of all peoples. With all its beauties and difficulties, with all its joys and sorrows, this bond is of a mysterious nature. Grounded in creation itself, its meaning and its goal far transcend the desire of the individual; its destined purpose and laws do not emanate from the individual but were there before him, and are of a higher order. The individual has merely the option, as with all obligations and tasks, of honestly fulfilling, or of not fulfilling, them.

We had nothing to do with our coming into this world, but once we are born, certain tasks and aims are allotted to us. Without our having any say in the matter, we were born either male or female in sex, but thereafter, whether we are a man or a woman, the duties pertaining to one or the other are assigned to us. We did not make the decision that mankind should be divided up into men and women and that only out of the union of man and woman could it continue. That is just the ways things are. Just as it was not we, but a higher Power who decided the question whether mankind be created and how it should be constituted, so also do the tasks arising from existence and the duality of sex transcend us.

Many people today, under the influence of that individualistic mentality of the not so distant past which regarded everything purely from the point of view of "in what way is this most agreeable and profitable to me," may find it difficult to recognize and believe in the sublimity of the eternal laws binding on mankind. Nevertheless, there it is—man is not his own master, he is limited, he controls neither his beginning nor his end, but is totally dependent; he is a creature and, as such, must perform the tasks assigned to him by the Creator.

It would be idle and presumptuous to quarrel with the Creator about this. It is humanly understandable that in moments of sorrow or suffering the anguished cry is wrung from the afflicted creature: "Why has all this happened, and why should everything be so difficult; why should we submit to laws which transcend us and which we may not alter in the least in our own favor?" Yet, however great our sympathy for afflicted humanity, we cannot evade facts—we are creatures, created, preserved, and finally recalled by a higher Power. From this Power comes our existence and from It also our destined end. . . . We are touching here on the great and difficult problems of existence—the Whence, the Where, and the Why. Despite all the efforts of the human intellect throughout the centuries to find an answer to these questions, men's feeble minds are still unable to penetrate the wall of mystery that surrounds these problems.

The ultimate elements of being are wrapped in mystery for us children of men. So also the fact of being a man or a woman, the division of mankind into two sexes orientated toward one another and fruitful when united in love, is, in the last analysis, something mysterious, a sphere reserved for the realization of God's special plans, and one which is under His very special protection. Let us stand in awe before the mystery which is man, woman, and child.

The man who chooses a wife takes to himself a creature of God. The woman who pledges herself to a man links her life to a creature of God. When they transmit life to a child, they are fulfilling, whether consciously or unconsciously, whether with or without consent, the plan of the Creator for the preservation and multiplication of the human race. They, by their fruitful act, transmit to the next generation that life which has come down to them as the result of a bond of love between man and woman having been renewed time and again during the course of thousands of years. The next generation will pass it on again to countless posterity, since the bond of love is being ever continued. Who could seriously believe that marriage is exclusively the private concern of husband and wife?

Compliance with the Creator's salutary laws increases our all-round stature. In the fulfillment of the duties which are implicit in being a man or a woman lies the means of evolution to a truly finer human race.

As a result of all these considerations, we object on principle to divorce and recommend that young people be brought up in the knowledge of the greatness and significance of the two-fold and yet common task of marriage—mutual formation and procreation. They should be prepared to enter the married state conscious of its great and difficult obligations, and with the firm resolution to perform these in a manner consonant with human dignity.

It is pure cowardice on the part of young people to close their eyes to the seriousness of life, to be unwilling to face the possible difficulties of marriage, and, instead of a genuine and indissoluble union, to contract a parody of it with the mental reservation that they will separate should difficulties arise. The spiritual basis of marriage is a conviction on the part of the couple that this union will further their mutual personal development and perfection, and an intention to show a true reciprocal regard for each other in the course of realizing a lasting and common achievement of value. Marriage ought to be contracted only in the awareness of its indissolubility and with the firm purpose to be faithful to the end. The mere thought of the possibility of divorce already holds a potentially dangerous invitation to untie the marriage bond.

There are also serious objections of a social nature to be brought against divorce. Through marriage, two people have placed the shaping of their lives on a new foundation. They have renounced much, given up many opportunities of ordering their lives differently, and staked all on a life with the chosen companion.

This transformation affects not only the psychological but the physical life, and also, very decisively, the economic and social living patterns of the couple. It would be an illusion to believe that simply by saying, "You can have your freedom," or, "I will have nothing more to do with you," one is released from one's obligations. When a divorce is forced on one of the partners, a grave injustice is done to the other, but to the wife particularly, for when she is old and toilworn it is difficult for her to find again a home, support, and security.

A great injustice is also done to the children, as they have a natural right to grow up in a normal family environment. In some particularly sad cases, it is sometimes better to take the children out of the unhealthy atmosphere of an unhappy marriage, but these cases are exceptions; they do not release society from its obligation to protect the innocent party and the children from the wrongdoing of the guilty party. The tasks of the married state are too exalted and too important to society to be left to the mercy of individual whim or passion. The State has not only the right but the obligation to protect marriage and the family. All authorities responsible for the common good, therefore, are bound to protect the interests of the innocent party and of the children.

In very exceptional cases a separation *a mensa et thoro*, which does not permit remarriage, may afford the best possible way out.

Those who speak so flippantly about the dissolution of marriage and about remarriage, would do well to consider the following: Anyone who speaks of marriage must at the same time think of a family. Anyone who discusses marriage without on principle including the family is not really talking of marriage, for the childless marriage (not in certain isolated cases but as an institution for mankind in general) is simply unthinkable, since if marriages were childless mankind would cease to be. The way of life of couples who refuse to have children is essentially their personal affair. The question will be solved automatically at their deaths, and in any event it is not a problem which interests society in general.

Marriage laws have meaning only insofar as on principle they take the family into consideration. Fully to cover the subject of marriage, they must be based on the concept of family and procreation.

The objection may be raised that, according to reliable figures, 10 per cent of all marriages are naturally sterile, besides which a great many others are compelled to remain sterile for various reasons. Must these blamelessly childless marriages be subject to the same stringent laws of permanent fidelity and indissolubility as apply logically to those fruitful ones which serve the community?

At all times races of low cultural standing have held to the view that fidelity and unity should apply to the fruitful couple only. We think differently. Although fruitfulness belongs essentially to marriage—considered as an institution serving mankind in general—yet fruitfulness is not conferred on each individual marriage. If the Creator withholds this blessing from particular marriages, this does not release the parties affected from the obligation to live according to the eternal laws for husband and wife. Their life must be a practical recognition that marriage has been instituted for man and not by him, and is permanent and indissoluble. That such childless marriages are not without value is something about which we shall speak at greater length later.

Only through proper training of the whole personality, which must begin in early youth, can matrimonial unhappiness really be avoided.

The fulfillment of the full potentialities of human nature demands far more than the mere exercise of instinct and feeling; it implies, above all, the exercise of reason and will, since these constitute the supreme faculties of man. We must remain conscious of our human dignity, which is of greater significance than sexual potency or having a large bank account.

Marriage is not merely a physical and economic union of two people of different sex, but is a natural vocation of mankind which far transcends a personal desire to enjoy life.

XII

CONTROLLED CONCEPTION

1. The growth of population

In the period between the two world wars, as a result of great economic crises in civilized countries, a general fall in the birth rate made itself apparent, and the danger of a decline in population was frequently overstressed. Developments in recent years, however, show that there are no grounds for anxiety on the score of the human race dying out.

Today large sections of people fear exactly the opposite. Great catastrophes are predicted for mankind if the growth of population is not radically checked. In wide and influential circles, the demand is being made for the prevention of births at any cost and by any means.

Let us seek to get a clear picture of the present situation, starting with this question: how many children, on the average, should there be in each family so that the population not only does not decline but increases moderately? That depends in the first place on the mortality rate which varies considerably at different periods and among different peoples. In every year the number of deaths should not only always be balanced by the number of births, but the latter should be even slightly in excess. The birth rate, therefore, must be constantly somewhat greater than the death rate. (Birth rate and mortality rate

151

are usually given per thousand of the population yearly.) If, for example, the present birth rate in Germany is given as 17 per thousand, that means that in every year 17 children are born alive there for every 1,000 inhabitants.

In previous centuries, the birth rate was very high and reached about 40—even 50—per thousand of the population. Even in the present day, there are still countries whose birth rates are between 40 and 50 per thousand, for example, China, Malaya, Venezuela, Mexico, Guatemala and some other Central American countries, as well as parts of Africa.

The mortality rate, however, was also very high in the past, being around 40 to 50 per thousand, so that the excess of births was always very small and worked out at only 2 to 3 per thousand, or at the very highest, 5 per thousand.

In the second half of the last century, the mortality rate began to fall rapidly and, up to the present time, a slow and constant decline has been maintained. Today the rate works out at an average of 9 to 10 per thousand and may well have reached its lowest level in the more advanced countries.

If, side by side with the prevailing heavy fall in the mortality rate, the birth rate had remained at the same high level as in the past, an enormous excess of births would have occurred, resulting rapidly in a huge overpopulation of civilized countries. This did not happen, however, for in a very short time a fall in the birth rate set in. In the beginning, it is true, the birth rate did not fall so rapidly as the death rate, so that, in spite of considerably fewer births, the excess of births over deaths was greater from year to year. Throughout the last century and up to the First World War, Europe experienced an increase of population to an extent never previously known. The population of Europe, which in 1800 was only 180 millions, had shot up to 460 millions at the start of the First World War (1914) and today amounts to more than 600 millions.

Although the birth rate has shown a big decline in all European countries, the excess of births is everywhere greater than in the centuries before 1800. It is between 4 and 6 per thousand in Austria, Belgium, Great Britain, Hungary, and Sweden; between 6 and 8 per thousand in Czechoslovakia, Denmark, France (7.1 per thousand), and Germany; between 8 and 10 per thousand in Bulgaria, Finland, Ireland, Italy, Norway, and Switzerland; between 10 and 12 per thousand in Greece; between 12 and 15 per thousand in Yugoslavia, the Netherlands, Portugal, Rumania, and Spain; 17.8 per thousand in Poland; 18.1 per thousand in the U.S.S.R.

At the present time, the average rate of increase for Europe as a whole amounts to 8 per thousand. This means that the European population at the present day has the tendency to increase from 620 millions to at least 1,500 millions in a hundred years. No one can, of course, say in advance whether this growth in population will actually take place.

In North America, the annual excess of births amounts to 16 per thousand, which includes the United States with 15.4 per thousand and Canada with 20 per thousand. If the current tendency is maintained, the population of North America will, in a hundred years, have increased fivefold.

Central America has an excess of 27 per thousand live births over deaths, Mexico alone having 32 per thousand.

South America has an excess of births of 23 per thousand, her population having a tendency, therefore, toward a tenfold increase in a hundred years.

If the population of Asia maintains its present excess birth rate of 18 per thousand, it will have increased six times in a hundred years. China, with a population of 690 millions, increases by 25 million annually. In Japan the excess is no greater than in Europe (10.5 per thousand).

Africa, whose birth rate is still 45 per thousand, has an excess of 19 per thousand, and her population should accordingly double itself in less than 40 years.

Australia has a population growth of 14 per thousand.

The birth rate is regrettably small in some large European cities.

The foregoing figures were taken from the *Demographic Yearbook of the United Nations*, 1959. In Fig. 43, we have sought to show vividly the evolutionary tendency of the world's

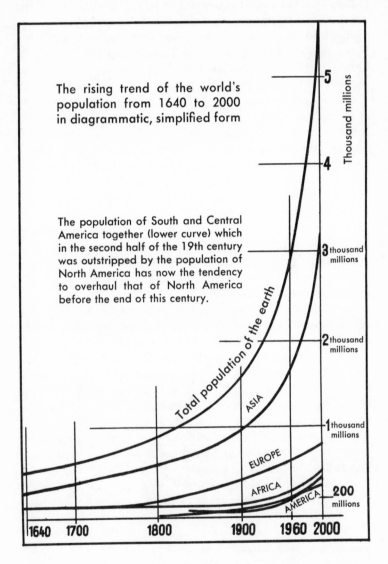

The rising trend of the world's population from 1640 to 2000 in diagrammatic, simplified form

The population of South and Central America together (lower curve) which in the second half of the 19th century was outstripped by the population of North America has now the tendency to overhaul that of North America before the end of this century.

Thousand millions

5

4

3 thousand millions

2 thousand millions

1 thousand millions

200 millions

Total population of the earth

ASIA

EUROPE

AFRICA

AMERICA

1640 1700 1800 1900 1960 2000

Fig. 43

population, but we would stress explicitly that we are in no way trying to predict how great the population will be in the years to come. It simply seemed to us sufficiently interesting to indicate the current evolutionary trend.

The total population of the world today (1961) amounts to about 2,900,000,000. The excess of births works out at an average of 17 per thousand, which is about triple the rate essential for the healthy and steady growth of mankind. The excess has never before been so high. If the present tendency is maintained, the population of the world will double itself in 40 years, and amount to about 6,000,000,000 around the year 2000. Toward 2040, it should double itself again and amount to about 12,000,000,000.

There is food for thought in the fact that mankind, in many thousands of years of existence, could not reach the 3 billion mark, but that it requires no more than 40 years to grow from this figure to 6 billion. Experts believe, however, that in those countries with a smaller population density and very high excess of births (Central and South America, China, and South West Asia, etc.) a decline in births will come with increased density exactly as happened in Europe in the recent past. It is estimated, therefore, that the population of the globe, toward the middle of the next century, will be only 6 to 8 billion instead of 12 billion.

We are of the opinion that the population should not double itself sooner than in 100 to 150 years. By present-day health standards, this corresponds to an average of 4 children per couple, that is, to an annual excess of births of 5 per thousand. To ensure the maintenance of a healthy and ample growth of population, it is therefore sufficient to utilize only about half the fertility potential in woman.

It follows very clearly from this that, from the social point of view, it is not expedient to take full advantage of female fertility. There is a general need to control the number of births in relation to the purely natural procreative potentiality. A conscientious regulation of the number of children in every marriage does not harm the interests of the nation.

In order to be able to pass judgment on birth control, two different problems, which unfortunately are very often confused, must be clearly distinguished:

1. Is it in the interest of the development of the nation or in the interest of the individual family necessary, desirable, or to be looked upon as the ideal, that *each married couple should produce the highest number of children of which they are physically capable?*

If full advantage were taken of female fertility, as is sometimes advocated in thoughtless circles, this would result in a doubling of the population in about 25 years and a sixteenfold increase in a hundred years.

Natural fertility would be capable of producing 8 or more children in every family. No person with any knowledge of demographic problems could seriously advocate such population growth. Inordinately large families are not the ideal.

In this sense, but in this sense only, do we advocate birth control, for we are of the opinion that order and conscientiousness are essential in the building up of family and society, and that, on this account, a restriction in the exploitation of fertility in keeping with the demands of these is necessary. This viewpoint may be described as the one generally accepted today.

At the same time, we stress emphatically that family and population growth should be normal and healthy. To any limitation of births which hinders this we are strongly opposed.

2. Today the regulation of the size of families must, on principle, be considered from a standpoint different from that formerly obtaining. Up to the present, the problem was first and foremost a moral one—the keeping of chastity. But today it is possible to limit the number of children without violation of conjugal morality, so that arguments hitherto advanced in behalf of complete abstinence have lost their general force (see Chapter XIII).

If one chooses the natural instead of the unnatural way, there is an advantage to which we shall refer in §4 of this chapter. If, furthermore, many families struggling hard for an economic existence now have less children, this is to be welcomed, for only the healthy family is the ideal one, and not the family in want and misery with too many children.

2. The normal family

Much ethnological research has shown that, among primitive people, nature herself takes care of the proper size of the family. A mother breast feeds her child for two or three years during which period she is sterile and menstruation does not occur. After a lapse of two or three years, the regular sexual relations of the couple result again in a pregnancy, and so it goes on up to the time of the woman's menopause, during which fertility comes to an end. Thus births follow one another at average intervals of three years. This—in the literal sense of the word— natural birth control corresponds to the healthy interests of the woman and avoids simultaneously an immoderate growth in family. At that primitive level of civilization, man has no need of conscious birth control; nature takes care of it alone.

Due to the influences of civilization, this natural birth control has been lost in the course of centuries. In civilized countries today, most women can become pregnant again three or six months after a confinement. Even the mother who is breast feeding her child does not usually remain sterile for long. Mostly after a few months, even during the lactation period, menstruation reappears, which is a sign that conception is again possible. But so quick a succession of births would soon exhaust the woman's strength, the family would become intolerably large, and the health of mother and child would be undermined; in addition, the general population would increase at an alarming rate.

As the action of nature, alone and without the conscious help of man, no longer suffices, it is the duty of civilized man, with greater rational judgment and more highly developed moral sense, to take deliberate and necessary action. Among civilized people today, there is no ideal of a "true to nature, normal family," such as has been demanded by many learned individuals. In place of this normal family of former times must come the family which is normal in respect of both nature and civilization.

Man is not a mere creature of nature, whose life and pattern of living are regulated solely by instinct and desire, as obtains in the irrational and instinct-dominated animal world. It is indeed precisely the hallmark of human activity that it rises above the laws of nature, dominates, directs, and regulates them, purposefully enlists the forces of nature in its service and employs them for its own ends. Undoubtedly man remains enormously dependent on nature; nonetheless he is neither blindly subject to her and her instincts nor powerless against her rule. Man is essentially a civilized being; that fact manifests itself in all his works and institutions, in the formation of his family, and in the evolutionary pattern of his society.

There is probably no sphere of general human activity and no human relationship in which the harmony of nature, civilization, and the supernatural is more important than in that of the sexual life and marriage. Man does not surrender blindly to impulse; instead he uses the powers of nature in accordance with the cultural character of his being and his mission, for the purpose of attaining supernatural values and aims. This applies very particularly to the sexual nature of mankind, and for him marriage is a sacrament.

It should, therefore, be regarded as self-evident and not as a subject for argument, that in the matter of the number of his children, and the time of their conception, civilized man will also be guided by rational and responsible considerations and will not, passively and stupidly, leave it to nature to fix the size of his family.

How large, then, should the normal family be? A family is of the right size when no injury is being inflicted upon the health of the mother or the children, and no obstacle is being put in the way of the capacity of each member of the family to develop materially and culturally, and when every family produces at least as many children as will ensure a constant, but not too rapid, increase in the general population.

As long as there are married couples who, as the result of

economic stress, are not in a position to support a normal family in accordance with their station in life, a betterment of economic conditions must be striven for by all possible means. Making it possible for each family to support four to five children must remain the fundamental consideration guiding all socio-political activity.

This is in no way to say that the number of children in each individual family should not exceed this number; we are concerned here only with a statistical average.

But besides the minimum demands, there must also be a place for the ideal. Minimum requirements are for mass performance. The ideal appeals to those who feel called to special tasks with all the attendant happiness, but also with all the difficulties and sacrifices entailed.

The question of the right number of children will, nowadays, frequently be answered thus: parents should give life to as many children as the living standard given by God to their family allows (according to Bishop Franz von Streng in his book *Geheimnis der Ehe—The Mystery of Marriage*). One can give parents no better and more sensible direction for their personal point of view and their individual line of conduct.

But social considerations will take us further than this, and the question must be asked as to whether, generally speaking, the existing living space at the command of parents is sufficient to enable them to have as many children as desirable from the social point of view. This poses a major problem of social policy. Everything must be done to make reasonably early marriages possible and to provide parents with accommodation (which they are generally unable to acquire by their own efforts) which would enable an average of at least four to five children to be maintained in each family.

3. The difficulties confronting healthy family development

Formerly it was possible to a great extent to adapt the living space and the level of subsistence to the size of the family. It is not the same today. As a result of the widespread division of labor, the individual no longer produces what he himself needs, but each one is, more or less, producing for the community, and as a consequence is dependent on others for the provision of his needs. In the cities especially, most people, whether salaried or contract workers, are in a permanent state of dependence in respect to their incomes. Those in receipt of a fixed remuneration cannot increase the amount of their earnings, or can do so only insignificantly, and hence are compelled to adapt the number of their children to the size of their incomes.

To an industrious mankind, nature offers in abundance all that it needs for existence. In order to avoid the problems attendant on relative overpopulation, therefore, it is essential that the production of goods, and above all their distribution, be organized in every state and between the individual states. There must also be assured to the population educational, housing, employment, and health facilities and services.

As the density of population increases, it is true these problems always become more difficult, because they demand changes in the world's social and economic structures and the setting up of new, large organizations. The interdependence of individuals and communities becomes greater in proportion as the population of the world becomes greater. In this evolutionary process, time and again difficulties are encountered which endanger the existence of individual families and entire nations, since the individual does not live on abstract potentialities but on solid reality with whatever that has to offer in the way of food, clothing, housing, and educational facilities. In this technical age, especially in densely populated areas, it follows that there is a demographic problem in a form never known in earlier centuries.

The strong tension in the basic relationship between the life force and the scope available to it is to be explained in part by the fact that the solution to social and economic problems is not generally sought until these latter, already grave, have assumed a menacing aspect. It is only in recent years that the practice has slowly grown of seeking some solution to social problems which are expected to arise in the near future, and of making preparation by paying attention to the present evolutionary trends. There come to mind the praiseworthy efforts of the various United Nations' organizations, such as, for example, the World Health Organization, or the Economic and Social Council.

Undoubtedly these efforts are limited. All the factors which later prove to be important cannot be included in the preparatory planning for the simple reason that they cannot be known in advance. Nobody would have been able to include the use of atomic energy in future planning so long as the way to the acquisition of nuclear energy had not been found. It is man's lot that he will never be the untrammeled master of his destiny, even in the era of the greatest technical development. "The poor you have always with you" (Matt. 26:11).

In many modern states, the public finance administration exercises a decisive influence on the possible size of the family, for upon it depends how much of the public income will be used for family assistance purposes. State policy in varying ways and in different measure can offer encouragement for the support of children in individual families, starting with marriage loans which would facilitate early marriages, and going on to family allowances, the creation of a family wage and educational grants. Effective family assistance can come through public health service, infant, sick, and old-age welfare, housebuilding and settlement, provision of employment and improvement of conditions among migrant workers.

With increasing population density, the need for more far-reaching social organizations becomes always greater, and the setting up and operation of them becomes increasingly more difficult. Simultaneously, the dependence of the individual on such economic organizations and their efficient running, when it comes to founding and maintaining a home, also increases.

Again, the difficult problem of the security of existence is not one which the individual can solve by himself. Never was mankind's anxiety about existence as acute as at the present time.

This is, of course, above all a religious problem and hence cannot be solved, in the first place nor exclusively, by economic measures.

It remains true, nevertheless, that the basic economic situation of a family is often dependent upon events and influences in regard to which the individual affected is powerless—economic crises, wars, political despotisms, mass concentration camps, racial persecution, mass deportations, expulsion or extermination of an entire people, and so on. The number of children or the density of population is, in its own way, a people's answer to the question of confidence in its future, even if the grounds for that confidence are objectively false. This was demonstrated, for example, in the increase in the number of children during the era of National Socialism which so grievously betrayed its adherents who followed it in blind credulity and, full of rosy expectations, unconcernedly brought children into the world. What tragedy was to befall so many of these families in 1945!

Present-day conditions make early marriages impossible in many cases, and compel a woman, even after her marriage, to work for a livelihood outside her home. We do not contest a woman's right to work outside her home, but we object to a wife being compelled to do so because of the insufficiency of her husband's income. In this age of "automation," it should be the first duty of the man, before seeking shorter working hours for himself, to relieve his wife from the necessity for breadwinning.

Early marriage is the most efficacious way of preventing excessive aging of a population. Unfortunately this is not yet everywhere realized. If educated middle-class people are not in a position to found a home until they are between 30 and 40 years of age, they are not going to have many children. At 40 years of age most of them ponder the point whether they should still have children because of their fear of not living to see them established in life. The drawbacks in this situation must be removed. By the age of 35, the parents should already have achieved the normal family of four to five children. It is worth considering that in a hundred years this would provide the world with an extra generation!

After the First World War, unemployment, or the threat of unemployment, was the principal cause of the fear of having children. Today in many countries the housing shortage is the greatest obstacle to normal family development.

There are other circumstances, less frequently encountered but nevertheless always socially important, which urge or compel married couples either temporarily or permanently to forego having children—for example, a wife's state of health. Undernourished or sickly women cannot stand up to the demands of pregnancy without some detriment to their health. Grave deficiencies in the structure of the body can make childbirth a direct danger to the life of the woman. Other grounds for making pregnancy undesirable for the time being are a recent birth or illness of the woman.

When a pregnancy must be avoided in marriage, a grave question weighs upon the minds of the couple: how is conception to be avoided without their conjugal life suffering serious damage? This is a fateful question for millions of people today, and they are not to be put off with a few soothing, consoling or noncommittal clichés. There is a serious problem here—probably one of the most serious of contemporary problems. The question is not merely one which concerns the personal happiness of an immense number of human beings, but one which profoundly affects civilized life in general, the physical, psychological, and moral health of mankind.

4. Existing methods for avoiding having children

a) *Permanent abstinence in marriage*

So long as the monthly process in the female body remained insufficiently investigated and in addition to ignorance much superstition prevailed, the only advice which could be given to married couples in difficult circumstances was that they should abstain completely from sexual intercourse. That in theory is undoubtedly the simplest solution. But is it simple in practice?

We must realize what is being expected from a married couple who are asked to live permanently continent. As we have already stressed, sexual intercourse belongs essentially to conjugal love. Especially during the early years is it of far-reaching importance in the physical and moral life of husband and wife and in the fashioning of the home. It helps to preserve and strengthen their spiritual union; it draws the married couple together and effects their mutual adjustment. On this account it is extremely difficult for married couples to feel that they are unable to enjoy the pleasure of sexual union. The spiritual union usually suffers as a result, and the marriage bond is often strained.

The natural force of desire makes abstinence for the couple a crushing burden which, the longer it is demanded, the more heavily it weighs upon them. As all tender demonstrations of love would but make abstinence more difficult, the couple must also forego these. The result is that vexation and irritability increase, as do also the dangers to family peace.

Abstinence in marriage cannot be compared with the celibacy of unmarried persons or with that of religious. The conditions in the married state are essentially different from those in pre-marital life or in the religious life.

The late Dr. Niedermeyer, a Catholic Viennese doctor and sociologist, wrote (admittedly in 1931) on this subject of marital abstinence as follows: "We are by no means unaware of the difficulties. They become greater the longer the abstinence lasts. We know that permanent abstinence can, for the physical as also for the spiritual union, be a heavy burden which many are not strong enough to bear. It is nothing short of heroism which is demanded from such married couples."

Dr. Smulders, the Dutch Catholic practitioner, has this to say in his book on periodic abstinence: "Why needlessly condemn just those couples who have been most tried in their married life to complete abstinence, as though it were a mere bagatelle?"

The Belgian Catholic Dr. Raoul de Guchteneere expressed himself as follows on this question:

Among married people the question is complicated by the force of the stimulation provided by the very presence of the spouse and by the customary intimacies which conjugal closeness takes for granted. The state of psychic neutrality, indispensable for a normal and prolonged exercise of continence, would be extremely difficult to achieve and would require unceasing vigilance. It would, in fact, imply the foregoing of familiarities, of the contacts likely to provoke sexual excitability. The absence of such precautions would condemn the people concerned to an expenditure of nervous energy incompatible with sound health. For it is obvious that the inhibition of the genetic desire becomes infinitely difficult when it has been allowed, through imprudent concessions, to assume frenzied proportions. The amount of nerve-impulse expended in these circumstances to regain exhausting control is a drain on the available capital (of a person). There would inevitably be a diminution of the potential for the other occasions in life. But in any case we know that the sexual element is an important factor in the realization of that intimate fusion of personalities which is one of the indispensable conditions for a genuine conjugal union. There is no doubt but that the reciprocal affection which unites the spouses should be based on mutual esteem and respect, strengthened by common aspirations and interests. These elements suffice perfectly in supporting a comradeship or an ordinary friendship, but seem in the majority of cases to be incapable of ensuring and maintaining that subtle adjustment which the balance and stability of life in common demand. The sublimation of the sexual instinct is not something which can be attained easily in the conjugal state: very often it would have to be satisfied merely with repressions, of a more or less painful nature, which are not altogether without drawbacks. . . . Absolute continence in marriage, maintained over a long period, is a difficult road, fraught with perils among which it is vital to know how to find one's way with prudence. It would only be advisable, medically speaking and for the average run of married people, in those very rare cases where the possibility of a new pregnancy would represent such a danger that the intermediary method of partial continence would turn out to be inadequate.[1]

Hitherto the tendency was always to leave this problem alone. One was afraid to face up to it because one was unable to supply a satisfactory answer.

There is no disputing the fact that abstinence is possible in marriage, but it is so difficult an undertaking that, generally speaking, only specially endowed and profoundly religious people can carry it out fully. It is not for the general mass of people.

Periodic abstinence, on the other hand, is demanded in every marriage, and couples can generally stand up to the demand more or less satisfactorily. It is quite different with abstinence permanently enforced as the result of external circumstances. This represents a grave interference in conjugal relations and a difficult moral test for the couple. Inherent in it is always the danger of moral defections, infidelity and disorganization of the marriage.

b) Artificial methods of birth prevention

In view of the great physical and psychological difficulties which permanent abstinence produces in a marriage, we could, on natural grounds, even while objecting on principle to these practices, have sympathy for those couples who have recourse to morally objectionable methods.

One of the most common moral aberrations in marriage is the interrupted sexual act. The man interrupts sexual union with the woman just before he reaches his climax and behaves so that the spermatozoa cannot reach the female organ but are dissipated otherwise.

A second, and likewise exceedingly common, unnatural method for preventing the sexual act resulting in conception

---

[1] Raoul de Guchteneere, *La limitation des naissances* (Brussels: Édition de la Cité Chrétienne, 1931), pp. 223–25.

is the employment of so-called "contraceptives," for the manu-
facture of which a great industry has already come into being.
Some of these contraceptives prevent the entrance of the spermatozoa into the female body (the rubber type, etc.); others
again, of the chemical type, deprive the sperm, through chemical action, of its natural fertilizing power.

Making every allowance for the distressing plight of married
couples we must, nevertheless, designate that which is unnatural as also being immoral. Both the interrupted sexual act
and the employment of contraceptives constitute a grave
offense against nature—i.e., an act of unnaturalness—and are
hence morally reprehensible and to be forbidden under all circumstances. It makes it easier for us to speak out thus—in spite
of the extremely difficult position in which some couples find
themselves—because we are able to show them a way out of
their plight which is better in every respect and to which no
moral objection can be raised.

We have already pointed out that the marital surrender is a
surrender in love. The interruption of the sexual act before the
climax of sensation has been reached demands on the part of
the man great attention and the exertion of will power, and
means consequently a turning aside from the full loving surrender. This unnaturalness is of so grave a kind that if it is
repeated often the nervous system of the man suffers damage.
The interrupted sexual act usually leaves the woman unsatisfied
but strongly excited, and her nervous system also suffers se-
verely as a result of this ill-usage. Her general well-being is
affected, and, after a period of time, short or long, she becomes
sexually cold and indifferent. Nature defends herself against
those who do violence to her. As a result of the woman's sexual coldness (frigidity), the psychological harmony of the
couple usually suffers as well. Because of the detrimental effects
on their health, a husband and wife generally cannot sustain
this unnatural practice for long, and for that reason they soon
seek another way out of the difficulty. If for them normal sexual
intercourse is not possible—or does not appear to be so—they
proceed to employ contraceptives.

In this practice there is also a grave interference in the natural processes, a disturbance of the course of nature. Above all, the use of contraceptive methods will be found highly distasteful by those whose sensibilities have not become blunted, while the sexual pleasure itself suffers very considerably through the applied type of contraceptive.

Whether by artificial means or by the interrupted sex act, the aim is to prevent the male spermatozoa penetrating into the female organism and there fertilizing the ovum, but the female organism is at the same time prevented from assimilating substances contained in the male sperm. Thus not only the primary but also the secondary purpose of conjugal intercourse is eliminated. The literal becoming one is not fulfilled, and the feeling of inner peace is disturbed.

The employment of contraceptives by the woman can bring about health troubles. It is immediately obvious that the constant use of chemically effective substances can scarcely continue without damage being done,[2] while the employment of the applied type of contraceptive frequently causes irritations and inflammations of the internal organs with possible grave results.

Upon the subject of the effect upon the health of normal and abnormal sexual intercourse Dr. De Guchteneere, whom we have quoted earlier, expresses himself at length in his work *La limitation des naissances*:

Whatever be the relative degree of effectiveness or of danger presented by the different contraceptive methods, they all fall indiscriminately under the one indictment. It has been long recognized that, independently of the fertilization which is its *raison d'être*,

[2] During recent years a lively interest has been taken in biochemical means which are to be made use of by the woman in the form of pills. Through their effect on the action of the glands of the hypophysis and of the ovaries, these substances are designed to prevent ovulation occurring during the period of treatment. Nature acts in a similar fashion herself in the case of the nursing mother. The treatment may be carried on for as long as one pleases throughout the years. We object to this method of direct sterilization as being contrary to nature. Moreover, no one today can say with certainty what effects upon the health may follow from such treatment, whether it be for the woman herself or for the offspring she may later have.

normal sexual intercourse has profound physiological repercussions, from which the female organism derives the chief benefit.

. . . During sexual intercourse certain male substances are assimilated by the female organs and carried into the blood stream, where, through the agency of the glands having internal secretion, they act as stimulants of the metabolism. Thus, to a large extent are to be explained the organic and psychic modifications of which marriage is so often the starting point in the young woman. . . . "The spermatic fluid plays an important dynamogenetic role in the woman" (Aragon).

Even Arbuthnot Lane, for all his neo-Malthusianism, believes in the beneficial effect of the absorption of the prostatic fluid for intestinal stasis and chronic mastitis.

This phenomenon of the spermatic assimilation, so long misunderstood, is no longer really doubted, especially since the researches of Professor Thomson in England and Doctors Vogt and Meyer in Germany. "It is perfectly well known and universally admitted that the female organism assimilates the spermatic products introduced after coition, and that these products have an action upon the woman whose development they assist, while the lack of them involves as many physical as psychic troubles" (Professor Laffont).

Dr. J. Sédillot, who has made a special study of this question, believes like Professor Laffont that the absence of the influence of the male sperm upon the woman is the cause of the many nervous and psychological disorders one so very frequently observes among women whose sexual intercourse is not natural.

To quote further from Dr. De Guchteneere:

The result of all this is that the use of contraceptive methods constitutes a very real denial of justice to the woman whom it deprives of the organic benefits which she has the right to expect from sexual intercourse.

The physiology of sexual intercourse, consequently, gives us a fresh confirmation of the principle enunciated earlier, which teaches that one does not, with impunity, deflect a natural function from the end to which it was assigned. And we may conclude with Sédillot that "every married woman who habitually indulges in preventive methods becomes, physiologically speaking, an abnormal being who may pay the penalty in her physical health and especially in her nervous endocrino-sympathetic balance."

W. Stemmer also (1940) stresses the beneficial effect of the male sperm on the female organism.

The main objection to the practical expediency of these contraceptive methods, however, is that they are not at all safe.

The safety of the interrupted sex act depends upon the man's capacity for self-control. Let his will power slacken only once and a conception can result.

There is in existence a vast literature upon the different types of contraceptives, yet in medical pronouncements the one verdict always recurs: "None of these means is absolutely safe; we know of no really safe contraceptive method." One need not be surprised, therefore, if some doctors go so far as to recommend the use of three methods at the one time.

The married couple who realize the insecurity of contraceptive means must thus live in constant uneasiness, as a result of which the wife often develops an anxiety neurosis.

As the need to limit the number of children affects above all the poor, a point in this connection must not go unnoticed—the question of cost. The use of artificial methods is expensive; for many, indeed, it is nothing short of prohibitive.

We see, therefore, that both the interrupted sex act, as also contraceptives, are completely unreliable ways out of the dilemma in which married couples find themselves. Both methods are first and foremost unsafe; in addition they are unhealthy and detrimental to the physical and psychological union of the couple, repulsive, expensive, and contrary to nature—hence morally reprehensible and nonpermissible. The Church condemns these perversions of nature as being grave sins.

c) Abortion

Taking into consideration the difficulty of complete abstinence and the insecurity of unnatural artificial methods, it is not to be wondered at that a couple often have an undesired conception. But to rid oneself of the unwanted pregnancy by means of abortion is abominable.

Anyone who is acquainted with human suffering and weakness will certainly have understanding for the plight of those who fall by the wayside. This must not, however, prevent us from rejecting in principle and condemning their wrongdoing for what it is. We do not wish to sit in judgment upon those who have become guilty of an offense as the result of distress or ignorance, yet we must rigorously, unequivocally, and resolutely reject the method of artificial interruption of pregnancy as a grave interference in the process of nature and in a separate human existence.

The child growing in the mother's womb is not an organ of the female body. The woman could not by herself produce a child. It must be generated by a man and a woman, and hence it is not a component part of the female organism but an individual living creature, a complete human being. It has already a body and an immortal soul, though its body is as yet undeveloped and it has no conscious knowledge of the outside world. Its position is similar to that of the newly born child which is also physically undeveloped and knows nothing of the world around it. The embryonic child is a full human being even if it must yet live in such intimate union with its mother and be unable to sustain life outside that union. It is precisely as much a child of the mother, only physically less developed, as the child already born, and has on that account exactly the same right to protection of its life as all other human beings. Already, from the first moment of conception, the child possesses human nature, even if the state does not accord to it legal-civil existence.

To contend that a woman has an absolute right over her own body and hence can get rid of an unwanted fetus is, consequently, erroneous. Apart from the fact that man has not the right to abuse, mutilate, or kill his own body, we are concerned here not with the individual body of the woman but with another human being. That this other human being does not as yet live among us is not to say that it does not exist before it is born. The human being is not created at birth but is merely released from its intimate living union with the mother and transported into different living conditions. In this question of abortion, an argument based on the sovereign right of the woman over her own body can only be maintained either through ignorance or bad faith.

The well-known English natural scientist, C. S. Sherington, in his book *Man and His Nature* (Cambridge University Press, 1942, p. 72), stresses emphatically that: "The child in its mother's womb is never, at any moment of its existence, a part of the mother nor a part of the maternal life."

In many newspapers there appear, in more or less veiled form, offers of "help" from quacks and midwives. In all countries various groups are striving to have abortion, up to now proscribed by the penal code as a grave offense, made freely available without penalty. Were this to come to pass, a grave disservice would certainly be done to women, and public standing would be given to the most unscrupulous persons.

Nature takes revenge for this interference in her activity. It can happen that many abortions are performed without any consequent ill effects whatsoever, yet grave danger is present in every case, and thousands of women annually pay with their lives for this interruption of a natural process. Very often the health is seriously impaired, there are illnesses of a temporary nature, or even the incapacity to bear a child to maturity. Worst of all for the woman, however, are the psychological effects of abortion. Experiences in recent years have been teaching us ever more clearly about the grave repercussions which— often making their appearance only years afterward—can affect the nervous system of the woman.

But even if no ill effects to health were to result from abortion, it would still be monstrous that a mother should permit her own child, which has lived in such an intimate union with her, to be killed.

The Catholic Church imposes her heaviest penalty—excommunication from the society of the Church—for abortion. According to Canon Law, persons concerned in an abortion may not receive absolution from an ordinary priest but only from a bishop or from a priest specially empowered by him (Code of

Canon Law, can. 2350, par. 1). This stern attitude on the part of the Church derives from the fact that, according to Catholic teaching, a child which dies unbaptized is forever deprived of that supernatural happiness which is attainable only by the baptized.

Various reasons are advanced for the justification of abortion. Above all reference is made to the economic plight of married people. We do not close our eyes to the economic distress which exists among wide sections of peoples, but economic grievances are not to be resolved by murder! If married couples are to be permitted to kill their unborn child, then they must equally be permitted to kill the child already born.

Economic miseries must be removed by economic measures. If many mothers, out of the despair brought about by economic misery, agree to abortion, then this is a grave indictment of existing social conditions. But it does not justify abortion.

Statistics have been compiled with the object of ascertaining how many women, suffering from certain diseases, die during pregnancy or shortly after childbirth. The compilers of these statistics try to prove that these women cannot bear a child since the existing statistics show the great probability that pregnancy, if it is not interrupted, must cost them their lives. The intention is to demonstrate by these statistics the need to make abortion legally available "on medical grounds" in specific cases and diseases. Yet these statistics contain a grave source of error; they fail to tell us whether the women who died during pregnancy or after childbirth would not have died from the particular disease without any pregnancy or as a result of an abortion.

To the objection that the number of abortions is incomparably greater than the number of those penalized for the offense, and that hence the section in question in the penal law should be repealed, it can be replied—by way of example—that the number of offenses against the property of others (embezzlements, larcenies, cheatings, frauds, etc.) is in still greater disproportion to the number of those convicted, and yet it would not occur to anyone to suggest that the appropriation to one's own use of another's property or cheating should be legally permitted.

Among other reasons advanced for the justification of abortion are the probability of hereditary taint being transmitted to the child or the getting rid of the fruit of rape, and other reasons of the kind. In all these cases the answer is quite clear: whatever the circumstances may be, murder cannot be justified. The unborn child, even with hereditary taint, has the very same right to have its life protected as has the unborn child without such taint, or as has the child already born.

It is also quite unsound to argue that it is better for the child, who is not loved by the parents before its birth, not to be born at all. Mostly parental love does not make its appearance until the child is born. Besides, it could be claimed with equal right that parents must be permitted to kill the children already born if they do not love them.

To those married couples who have good grounds for wishing to avoid conception, but who do not wish to live in a state of complete continence, there remains only the solution of periodic abstinence as described in this book.

XIII

MORALS AND THE AVOIDANCE
OF CONCEPTION

1. Sexual stress

Man and woman were created for one another. They are by nature complementary to one another physically and spiritually, they are called upon to bear jointly the burden of a common task, and they have a natural right to live together. It is in accordance with the will of the Creator that they find one another, complete one another, and together become fruitful. Corresponding in the will of God to this fundamental (objective) co-ordination of the sexes is the force of the impulse (subjective) in the life of the individual being which urges him to seek union with another.

Human existence of itself, however, does not proceed from nature to a more perfect state. Man is not chiefly guided by nature. As a civilized being, he must employ both his creative power and his will power, and he stands in need of grace and blessing from above. This applies especially to his married life. The union of man and woman brings with it ties, obligations, and burdens which are often difficult to bear and which in some circumstances of life seem utterly intolerable.

The natural capacity for sexual activity is, in its fulfillment, inseparable first and foremost from the consent of another being, a person of the opposite sex whose dignity must be re-

spected and preserved at all times. Cohabitation and the creation of new life bring with them personal and material (economic) obligations, and it is taken for granted that a couple
start off with reasonably good health. The marriage bond frequently presents the partners with grave and difficult problems.

The strains and hardships which on the one hand result
from the strength of desire, and, on the other, from the difficult
performance of the obligations attached to the conjugal state,
have frequently been discussed under the name of "sexual
stress." Wherever distress makes itself felt oppressively, there
occurs, as a result of the weakness of human nature, the tendency to obliterate moral barriers, to declare permissible that
which cannot be permitted, and to brand the incorruptible
champions of law and of convention as pitiless, cruel, or un-
worldly interpreters of the strict letter of the law. It is more
agreeable to lay down demands which are comparatively easy
to fulfill than those which are difficult. In fact, the demands of
the moral law are often hard in practice.

Nature does not make us a present of harmony ready made.
On the contrary, man himself, by deliberate moral effort, must
aspire to it, through struggle and sacrifice. Man cannot suffer
himself to be guided merely by conative nature. His dignity is
founded rather on the spiritual part of his nature, on his vocation to a higher standard, which means nothing other than the
collaboration of man in the plans of the Creator. Human nature achieves its supreme expression under the benign influence
of the supernatural.

Only to those of profound insight does the overwhelming
truth reveal itself that the moral laws represent the expression
of the divine harmony in human nature as a whole; that their
fulfillment—in spite of all the hardships involved—does not at
all increase earthly evil but rather reduces it as much as possible. On the contrary, any deviation from the moral standard
increases the evil in the world, even if at first it appears as an
alleviation of the personal distress of the moment.

It can happen that many people who, in situations of grave
stress, advocate deviations from the moral law do so, in fact, in

good faith. They mean to do right because they are above all striving for some good, namely an amelioration of an immediate emergency. Yet these people err, for each deviation from the moral law—in spite of temporary relief—has evil consequences in the end.

The efforts to relieve sexual crises or the difficulties of married life by nonpermissible methods include all the unnatural, artificial, contraceptive practices already described, and abortion. Distressing circumstances make the doing of many things—humanly speaking—understandable, but they do not justify them.

Formerly, when the natural way of avoiding conception was unknown, prevention of conception was in all cases assumed to be a disturbance of the natural order. Such an interference in nature was consistently rejected as morally reprehensible in ethically minded circles, most categorically and resolutely by the Catholic Church.

Today, however, we are faced with a new situation: there exists a way of avoiding conception without disturbance of the natural order, and this way is morally unobjectionable. As a result of a set habit of thought, many people, who do not perceive the altered circumstances clearly, find it difficult to understand that—according to the way in which an aim is to be achieved—a distinction must be drawn between a natural and morally permissible method of avoiding conception and an unnatural and morally reprehensible method of preventing conception. They believe that both the one and the other method must in equal measure be morally permissible or morally objectionable. Let us, therefore, examine this question.

2. Marriage and the duty of procreation

To the natural right of married couples to sexual life together, there belongs too the duty to fulfill the meaning of conjugal cohabitation. Marriage and procreation are most intimately linked together. Outside of marriage, sexual intercourse and procreation are not permissible.

The ethical systems of nearly all civilized peoples are in accord with this high tenet of Christianity. It forms—as do monotheism and the concept of property—one of the ethical foundations upon which human society rests.

It is undoubtedly true that in each new generation, in the constantly repeated struggles for the practical realization of this principle, mankind must suffer innumerable departures and deviations from this high ideal. This belongs to the tragedy of human existence, but it in no way changes the rightness of the high moral principle. Generation and sexual intercourse are morally permissible only within the bond of permanent and indissoluble monogamy. It follows from this that implicit in marriage, as an institution embracing mankind, is the duty to procreate.

Highly as we rate procreation, however, we must not place it higher than marriage itself. Morally, procreation remains absolutely bound up with the bond of marriage. Hence its separation from marriage—on political or other grounds—may not be advocated. Furthermore, the bond of marriage is too strong and its natural and supernatural value too high for it to be loosened because of an unfulfilled desire for children. A marriage may not be dissolved even when, in the course of conjugal cohabitation, it becomes evident that it will not be blessed with children. Neither, in such cases, is it permissible to have recourse to artificial insemination. Nothing at all justifies this wrong method for which the sensation-mongering press has worked up interest through wide publicity and which presupposes the debasement of a man's dignity.

That procreation is the normal end in marriage is both in accordance with the general conviction of all ethically minded persons, and also with our natural feelings. It is good and desirable, and should of itself be a first and natural outcome of every marriage, for it is the natural fulfillment of the meaning of the conjugal union, and a joy and blessing for the parents. Through marriage, the couple have themselves voluntarily undertaken the privileges and the tasks of the married state and with them, therefore, the great and important task of providing for the continuance of the human race. Among the duties of the married state is that of procreation which gives—within the framework of the total task confronting us—valuable substance to our lives.

The transmission of life is an act of great value. In the hostile atmosphere of the present day, we must learn to recognize this value, to affirm it and to hold fast to it. The rearing of children, their spiritual, moral, and religious education, the molding of them into upright, useful, and worthwhile men and women is a lofty and valuable undertaking. It increases the inner worth of the parents and society benefits thereby. For the majority of people, the marriage blessed with children is the natural one which enables them to put to the most fruitful advantage the talents with which the Creator has endowed them.

Among people of moral outlook, no doubt exists but that the begetting of children and their formation into valuable individuals belong in the normal way to the tasks and merits of marriage. This in no wise means—as we have already stated in earlier sections—that the begetting of as many children as is physically possible belongs to the duties of marriage.

Even if it were possible for all married couples to maintain a normal family, this would in practice mean that only a small part, scarcely a half, of the natural fertility available would be utilized. According to Bishop Franz von Streng, parents should have as many children as the living space given by God to their family permits.

Although the marriage blessed with children is the normal and desirable one, and the one which alone fulfills the main purpose of marriage, yet, according to the general consensus of authorities on ethics, no absolute obligation exists for every individual marriage to produce children. (Only in respect of the other partner does the obligation to procreate exist for each married couple, supposing it to be demanded as a right by the other.) Were the renunciation of procreation in marriage immoral in itself, complete abstinence in marriage would not be permissible either.

For many—indeed for most—married couples today, a certain

limitation of births is simply essential. Only a few couples are able to give free rein to the impulses of nature in this question of procreation. To how many—or how few—children the fertility of the individual marriage will be limited is not of itself, nor primarily, a question of chastity (it can be this of course in addition) but rather one of conscious responsibility for one's whole life.

Not every renunciation of children is morally justified. Unfortunately, motives of a mean kind can be at the root of it. There must be no mistake, either, about the fact that among young married people very considerable ignorance prevails in the matter of the creation of a family—most of them are unaware of the happiness they are denying themselves by abstaining from having children. Formerly, comfort and vanity were often the considerations which, in many social circles, kept the size of the family small. As a result of social changes, these ignoble motives no longer hold pride of place. Today it is rather the passion for all those things that modern technology and civilization have to offer which is standing in the way of the enlargement of the family.

But in many cases, notwithstanding the best intentions of the married couple, external difficulties over which they have no control make it imperative that they limit the number of their children. Such difficulties could be, for example, legitimate anxiety in respect of financial security, late opportunity for marriage, employment of wife, lack of housing, sickness, unemployment, insufficient income, poor food supply, permanently bad health, or certain hereditary dispositions.

There is no doubt that in all such cases the limitation of the number of children, and with that the avoidance of conception, is morally permissible.

3. The two ends of marriage

What should—and must—married people do who wish to avoid a conception? Many people reply that in such cases married couples are bound to live in a state of complete abstinence. We, on the contrary, hold the view that couples in such cases cannot be asked to forego their natural right to the most intimate union, which has furthermore been sanctified by the sacrament of matrimony. Rather do we believe that periodic abstinence—that is, abstinence on the wife's fertile days—suffices.

If married people, by mutual agreement, wish to live in a state of abstinence, that is their own personal affair, and no one has the right to interfere. We are opposed, however, to those who lightly take it upon themselves to demand that people should practice complete abstinence in their marriage for years merely because they themselves are of the private opinion that this course is morally superior, or the only one in keeping with human dignity, etc., as this sort of empty claptrap always runs.

No one has the right to impose such a demand upon another. We must rather respect the right of married persons to their conjugal union, for it is a natural right, that is to say, a God-given one. It does not originate with man, and hence man cannot suspend it. Not even one of the spouses may demand total abstinence from the other without any imperative reason and against the other's will, for by virtue of the matrimonial consent each has bound himself or herself to fulfill the conjugal duties. Anyone who regards permanent abstinence in marriage as a higher state of perfection may pursue this way, provided that the other partner is of the very same opinion, but there must be willingness to respect the opinion of those who think differently. We are convinced that people who wish to live permanently in total abstinence have missed their vocation in getting married; instead of marriage they should have chosen the single state in order to achieve the higher merits desired.

One may not without good reason demand from married couples, as a "way to perfection," a line of conduct which is contrary to the meaning of marriage. In many cases enforced abstinence in marriage not only does not aid in perfection but rather results in a danger to morals.

As a most intimate partnership of life and love, marriage

does not lose its meaning if its primary end, procreation, cannot be fulfilled either temporarily or ever. The importance of marriage for the human race does not consist in the absolute requirement that each individual married couple should propagate. The species is not dependent for its preservation upon the fertility of every individual marriage.

Marriage and the conjugal union possess a twofold character. This was always the teaching of moralists when they spoke of the primary and secondary ends of marriage. The first and primary end of marriage is the propagation of the species. The secondary ends are the practice and preservation of mutual love and faithfulness, and the satisfaction of desire. We today understand this double aspect better as we now know that healthy nature has been so created by God as to achieve both ends of marriage. Nature has assigned days for procreation; she has assigned substantially more days for the realization of the secondary ends of marriage and on these days procreation is not possible. We have already indicated earlier (Chapter XII, §9) how important from the physiological point of view is the fulfilling of the secondary ends of marriage.

The secondary ends in marriage are not in every respect subordinate to the primary end of procreation. They can be realized on the greatest number of days without the fulfillment of the main object. On these "sterile" days, they are the only end assigned by nature to the particular act of sexual intercourse. Thus they rank equal at times to the primary end. Nevertheless, as moralists have always taught, they remain essentially subordinated to the primary purpose, not indeed at the times of their realization during the course of the marriage but in their belonging essentially to marriage. That is to say: Without marriage and its primary end, these secondary ends would either not have been instituted at all by the Creator or at least not in this way—that is, they would at least not have had to be realized by the way of physical union. On that account sexual intercourse outside marriage, just for the sake of these secondary ends, is, according to the general consensus of opinion, immoral and unlawful. As an institution and by its nature, marriage is designed first and all the time for the primary end of procreation even if in individual cases this end cannot be accomplished. Only those who accept marriage for what it is, with all its tasks and duties, have the right of access also to its secondary ends. The actual independence at times of the secondary ends, their equal ranking at these times with the primary end, argues nothing against their essential (ontological) subordination to the primary end, procreation.

In spite of their essential subordination to the primary end, the secondary ends lose none of their great importance. If there are grounds against procreation, all this means for reasonable human beings is that abstinence is simply confined to those days which have been assigned by nature for procreation. But this does not at all mean that abstinence should be practiced on those days which have been assigned by nature not for procreative purposes but for the fulfillment of the secondary ends. According to the general teaching of moralists, sexual intercourse in marriage is of itself a morally good action. It has been sanctified by the bond of matrimony. It would not be understandable, and it is certainly not self-evident, that its omission on those days on which no compelling reason exists for practicing abstinence, should be of itself morally more perfect and more in keeping with human dignity than its performance. Voluntary abstinence in marriage resulting from some additional motive of a higher kind—for example, abstinence on religious grounds—can, of course, be the source of special moral merit.

4.   The end does not justify the means

If it is agreed that a certain amount of limitation of births is in itself permissible and under present-day circumstances often essential, and if it is further agreed that the avoidance of conception does not necessarily have to mean total abstinence, why then, ask many people, the "prejudice" against contraceptives? Why should one method be recommended and another declared to be morally objectionable? Is there not a contradiction here? Surely, when in all cases the object is the same, isn't the question of the "how" quite immaterial and a purely personal concern? Is periodic abstinence morally more permissible than every artificial method or perversion of nature in some other way? To draw a moral distinction between a natural method of avoidance of conception through "artful" periodic abstinence, and an unnatural method of preventing conception through a disturbance of the natural course of the sexual processes seems, to many, a piece of casuistical reasoning. Sophistry, a double morality, an ignoble mental attitude, insincerity—thus run the reproaches of our opponents. How the purpose is achieved is immaterial, the only question that matters is whether the method used to achieve it is safe.

Is it really of no consequence how one gains one's end? It is a fact, for example, that we must eat in order to live, and that in order to provide for our needs we must work. Those who maintain that the means used to gain one's end is immaterial must maintain the following sophism: If the main point, the end, is for us to live, then it is not important whether we earn our living honestly or dishonestly; we may therefore rob or steal.

The greatest evil of our time is the belief that, for the attainment of an end lawful in itself, any method that is technically suitable may be employed; the method chosen is immaterial—the end will justify it. During recent years this pernicious tenet has plunged mankind into the greatest misery. What, in the last analysis, constitutes the unbridgeable gap between all political heresies and the teaching of Christianity is this attitude to means. No end, however good, important, and noble justifies a method which is bad in itself. That is a tenet of Christianity which has been the teaching of the Catholic Church always and everywhere. That is also the teaching of every Catholic religious order without exception. It is remarkable that one can still hear the widely spread and false assertion that the Society of Jesus teaches differently. There is no Catholic, no priest, no religious, and no lay person who in this fundamental question can or may teach anything different. For an action to be morally lawful, end and method must first be free from all objection. An action which is morally lawful in itself obtains its moral good and blessing from the personal motives of the doer.

In scholastic moral philosophy this principle is usually expressed in the following way: *Bonum ex integra causa, malum ex quolibet defectu.* That is to say, an action is morally good if the entire thing (*integra causa*) is good: the substance of the action itself, its end, the circumstances of place and time, and the interior motives. If even one of these elements is bad, then the whole action is bad. Furthermore, the degree of the deficiency can affect the badness of the action.

This principle holds good for life in general and therefore for marriage. When it has been established that a conception must be avoided, there yet remains the question of the lawfulness of the method to be followed for avoiding conception. In our case the method is the practice of abstinence on the fertile days; but on the sterile days, the married couple may have normal and natural intercourse and thus attain fully and completely the ends of marriage which healthy nature herself provided for these days. In this line of action there is no perversion of the natural order, but merely a temporary foregoing of the conjugal union, permissible in itself and which is required by force of outside circumstances.

In the employment of contraceptive methods, however, or the interruption of the sex act, the question is not one of complying with the purposes of healthy nature, but of disturbing the natural processes. The natural ends, to the fulfillment of which sexual intercourse on these days is assigned, are defeated.

This difference has not only a moral character. The unnatural method disturbs the happiness of the couple, more or less adversely affects their health, and is repulsive. If the achievement of the secondary ends of marriage had not been so important to nature, she would not have made the sterile days in women so numerous. Sexual intercourse during the sterile days, therefore, is in full conformity with nature and with the designs of nature.

The intrinsic evil of unnatural birth-control methods is not due to the parents' desire to have no more children, but to the use of their conjugal rights in an unnatural way. This misuse of sexual power can also bring about physical and psychological damage, a consequence from which periodic abstinence is completely free.

5. The danger of misuse

One frequently hears the view expressed that, while periodic abstinence is undoubtedly morally lawful where the number of children must be limited, nevertheless it is better that knowledge of the method should be suppressed because of the danger it may be misused. For if it is so simple, it is contended, will not some married couples decide to have no more children even when they have no compelling reason for a limitation of the size of their family?

To this one can reply: If in these cases unnatural sexual intercourse is replaced by periodic natural intercourse, this reversion to naturalness can be regarded as a gain, and hence signify at least the lesser evil. But today it is certainly not the people in affluent circumstances and determined not to take upon themselves the burdens of parenthood who constitute the most urgent social problem. Rather must we now consider first those who, suffering under the heavy pressure of circumstances, await the knowledge of the solution which the Creator Himself has implanted in nature. If we accept the ideal of the progress of mankind, and if we would not see this ideal held back, we cannot renounce progress, however tragic the consequences of its misuse often are. In order to prevent the misuse of the new knowledge, we must do everything that we can to contribute to the awakening of good will and the cultivation of the right moral attitude.

This point of view must extend to the danger of a misuse of

intercourse outside marriage. One need not, however, over-estimate this danger, for the method under consideration is little suited for intercourse outside marriage as it demands a lengthy period of mutual adjustment (see Chapter VI, §4 a).

6. Conclusion

To sum up, it has been established that the abstinence from sexual relations during the woman's fertile days to avoid conception in marriage is not of itself unlawful. The deliberate use of the rhythm method is incontestably lawful in all cases in which it is "indicated," that is to say, in all cases in which the married couple have paramount reasons for avoiding a pregnancy or a further pregnancy, for example, economic reasons, poor health, the danger of transmitting hereditary deficiencies, and the impossibility of providing the children with a proper education.[1]

[1] See in this connection the clear attitude of Pope Pius XII as expressed in his much-quoted address of October 29, 1951 (*Discorsi e radiomessagi di Sua Santità Pio XII*, Tipografia Poliglotta Vaticana, vol. XIII, 333), and his address in French to specialists in hematology on September 13, 1958 (*Osservatore Romano*, September 15, 1958).

XIV

THE FUTURE OF THE FAMILY
AND POPULATION

1. Moral intention and economic capability

As we have already stated in earlier sections, moralists teach that the deliberate restriction of conjugal intercourse to the sterile days for the purpose of avoiding conception in marriage is morally justified only when, in each individual case, sufficient grounds ("indications") for avoiding conception are present— for example, health difficulties or economic considerations.

The increasing numbers of the population, its progressive density rate, the constantly growing interdependence of individuals on each other and the increasing dependence of the individual upon the community, especially in industrial countries with already high population density and small mortality rate—all these constitute new factors. And the new situation created by these factors means that nowadays points of view very different from those prevailing in earlier periods of man's history must be of decisive importance. A solution of the problem to which no objections can be raised must always take into account the general situation prevailing and at the same time leave the basic moral principles untouched.

Sometimes morally high-minded persons raise objections to the new method not because of any anxiety as to its resulting in too few children being born into the world, but because they

188

feel that the utilization of the sterile days favors man's pleasure-seeking propensity.

Experience teaches that the difficulties of life serve to spur men on to greater efforts to overcome them. Undoubtedly men increase their personal worth when in crucial situations they remain faithful to their convictions, and when they recognize the obligatory character of the moral laws even when these entail hardships and difficulties. When, especially, in the most intimate sphere of their lives and remote from all outside influence, a man and woman confront each other in full responsibility, their steady determination to bear the sacrifices demanded by the moral law cannot be without great importance for the development of character and personality. Readiness for sacrifice, self-control, and reverence for the moral laws are values without which there can be no civilization. But restraint can never be an end in itself, for experience likewise teaches that many, perhaps even most, people give up when the test becomes too severe.

We believe that the utilization of the sterile days, which demands from married couples abstinence on 18 to 20 days in the month (the first 5 days of the cycle and roughly 14 days around the middle of the cycle) does not favor the search for pleasure but presupposes a fundamental moral outlook and amounts to a severe test of character.

Moral intention and economic capability: these are the twin supports indispensable for securing the future of our population. Moral intention is a question which concerns the individual conscience; it must be solved by educational direction. Economic capability is a problem which must be solved by the power potential of our society.

Today the fate of the family is not for the most part dependent upon the will of the individual. Hence the population problem cannot mainly or solely be solved by the conscience of the individual.

In judging this problem of births, therefore, one should give more thought to the state of dependency of the individual and the often desperate struggle of men for some small place among the breadwinners, and not always blame the conscience of the individual for the small numbers of children or attribute childlessness to a general reluctance to make sacrifices and to pleasure seeking. The positive co-operation of the individual is certainly quite indispensable in tackling this problem, but nothing is to be gained by unjustified reproaches—far from helping, in fact, they only create resentment.

The task of providing the family with the living space to which it has a natural right devolves today in the first place on those who control major world affairs, those who direct the economy and the life of countries.

Two measures of a socio-economic nature must be put into effect for the assistance of the family: firstly, there must be an adequate income which is at least sufficient to enable a normal family to be maintained in a way suitable to their station in life; secondly, there must be security of existence so that one is not at the mercy of passing contingencies. On the economic level, in fact, procreation is allied to the confidence one can place in the future. For parents to feel security in regard to the future, insofar as it is possible to ensure it, in order to maintain and educate their children, is the most important condition for an increase in population.

The probability of healthier and more talented people being born increases with the birth rate, but of course the probability is so much the greater the more people of healthy stock and the less those of unhealthy stock propagate. For the national well-being, the relative number of healthy people is of decisive importance.

Nevertheless one must beware of falling into the grave error of believing that quality can be bred merely through reduction in the number and better rearing of the coming generation. Talents may not be bred; they are a gift from the Creator. It is true, of course, that their development and unfolding is dependent upon environment. Hence extra care with infants is highly desirable. Infant welfare and the decrease in child mortality are two especially welcome developments, as it was a waste of healthy energy on the part of people to bring many children into the world only to see them die immediately.

On the other hand, the basic economic demands of the family must not be exaggerated. It is a mistake and mostly only cowardly self-deception to declare that if one cannot give a child everything, it is better to have no child. Had our parents thought along these lines, none of us would have been born, for each one of us had to do without quite a lot. Those who have been reared in luxury are not always the happiest, and certainly not the best, of mankind. Careful character formation and training for a vocation are more valuable for the child than the inheritance of great wealth. Those who have accomplished most for mankind have nearly all come from poor families.

The growing interdependence of one individual upon the other has brought with it the danger of uniformity. For this reason it has fallen to the lot of the home and the family to remain at the present time a center for the development and unfolding of the personality. The individual home affords the opportunity, in the midst of an affectionate community, for the calling forth and fostering of personal values. The general increase in the number of children in recent years may well be connected with an appreciation of this fact and, in any case, is not explainable solely on the grounds of state aid to families.

Even the best economic conditions cannot produce the desire to have children; they can merely assist and facilitate this outcome, for parents must also have a proper outlook in life in order to overcome the individual desire for personal comfort. Hence it is the duty of the state to do everything within its power to safeguard and assist a healthy and natural desire for children and family.

As willingness to make sacrifices, morality, and the wish for children, all ideal prerequisites for the formation of a healthy family, are very definitely aroused and assisted by religion, the special duty devolves on the state, on these grounds, of protecting and assisting its religious groups.

Although the desire for the preservation of a particular race or people may be for some an effective incentive to procreate, the Christian-religious motive is, in all respects, the noblest and loftiest. Only those who know how to value the worth of the human soul, so intimately bound up with the body in its creation, will have access to the most profound motives for procreation.

2. Importance to society of behaving in conformity with healthy nature

If we wish to discover and to estimate the social importance of periodic abstinence we must ask ourselves whether, and to what extent, this method is suitable for affording orderly sexual relief to wide sections of the community and thereby preventing unlawful eruptions of sexual desire with their grave and injurious consequences.

Although there are many marriages today which are free from unnatural practices, in nearly all extramarital sexual relations recourse is had to unnatural methods. We have already referred to the health troubles which certain contraceptive practices can bring in their train.

The injurious effect of an unnatural sex life upon the moral behavior and development of individuals appears to us to be of more importance, nevertheless, than the damages it causes to health. Anyone who really is aware of the impurity and unlawfulness of unnatural sexual intercourse, but nevertheless continues with it, has his psychological equilibrium upset because he is acting against his better judgment. As the wrongful action is not confined to one single instance but, generally, is constantly recurring, all moral effort is thereby disturbed or repressed.

If the new biological discoveries now help to restore a healthy naturalness into the sex life of the majority of people, then they must be regarded as having the effect on society—which today is positively poisoned by artificial methods—of a purifying bath. We regard as the main advantage of the new knowledge the fact that it makes it possible for a married couple to satisfy their healthy sexual desire without imposing on them intolerable sacrifices. Mankind is thereby kept in closer touch with healthy nature, and the married couple, preserved from so many psychological upsets, remain in a state of receptiveness for the realization of higher values.

The most hideous blot on our "civilization" is the active destruction of the unborn in thousands and millions.

How great is the importance of knowing the fertile and sterile days of the woman in every individual marriage emerges from the following consideration:

If we assume that a woman gets married at the average age of 22 years and that she ceases to be fertile at the age of 46, then she is fertile during 24 years of her married life. Taking the number of children in the normal family as averaging five —a sociologist will scarcely dare to demand more as the average—then the total period of the five pregnancies amounts to not quite four years of married life. Let us assume further that the woman is sterile for a few months during lactation after each confinement (a belief to which we do not at all subscribe), and so we finally arrive at the figure that pregnancies and everything involved therewith account for a space of five to six years.

Taking into account that during these periods (during the last months of pregnancy and the weeks of confinement), abstinence of some length must be practiced, there still remain more than 18 years of fertility in the marriage.

What is to be done during this time?

Experience during recent times has taught us just what is being done. We need not expatiate. A quite small section only of married couples are able to muster sufficient moral courage to practice abstinence for the 14 to 18 years which lie between the first and final pregnancy and the definite arrival of the climacteric years.

From the point of view of society, the importance of the service rendered to procreation by this new biological discovery must not be underestimated. For if children are desired, a married couple, fully conscious of their responsibility and at a time when physically and psychologically they are in good health, can have sexual relations during the fertile period with the probability of producing healthy offspring (see Chapter VI, §5).

The procreation of new human beings now becomes a deliberate affair; it is "controlled." Man has subjected a domain of nature to his authority. What hitherto had perforce been considered a fantastic aspiration has become a reality: sexual intercourse can take place in a natural way without procreation and without transgression of the moral law. As a result, it has become possible, more than ever before, deliberately to place conjugal intimacy at the service of a loving marital union; but, most undoubtedly, there has also been laid a heavier responsibility upon the individual for the fulfillment of the ends of the marital vocation.

That there exists between man and woman a state of attraction, that they discover one another in love, form a marital union, and in an orderly conjugal life together find sexual relief, is in keeping with the healthy nature of mankind. Those responsible for the education of the people must ensure that no unnecessary obstacles stand in the way of this orderly, natural method of satisfying sexual desire.

When the natural satisfaction of the demands made by the instincts of self-preservation and sex are rendered unduly difficult or impossible for large sections of the population, the strength of the instincts inevitably results in unhealthy reactionary manifestations. Self-satisfaction, premarital sexual intercourse with frequent change of partner, and adultery are common outlet manifestations of the repressed sexual power clamoring for relief. As consequences of these outlets, we have illegitimate births, perversions, pregnancies made intolerable on economic or health grounds, and the killing of the unborn. Further consequences take the form of grave breakdowns in health, psychological upsets, nervous ailments, diminished capacity for true love with resultant lessening of the probability of healthy and happy marriages. The problem of sex is not a mere question of desire and temptation as small and narrow minds so often see it; it is a cultural and social problem of the greatest magnitude which has affected man at every stage of his history.

We are aware, of course, that it can be quite different in individual cases and that there are those people who, in their efforts to achieve a higher state of perfection and holiness, voluntarily give up marriage and the possession of earthly goods in order to develop their spiritual powers, free from outside disturbances and influences. But they are the exceptions; they are an elite. Their number is infinitesimally small in comparison with the large number of people whose inclinations are more natural and less supernatural. So although we should value very highly indeed the importance to society of these heroic persons, we must yet not judge people in general by these standards.

The search for a method which will enable all people to satisfy their natural desires in a normal way in keeping with human dignity is a great social problem upon the solution of which much depends for the future of our population.

Let us endeavor to draw some conclusions in regard to future developments from certain tendencies which are already apparent today.

In 1957 the United Nations drew attention to the upsurge in the population of the world which must, if the present annual excess birth rate of 16 per thousand continues, double itself within 40 years and quadruple itself within 80 years. The entire world press seized eagerly upon the theme and has continued to pursue it with further and further details. The astounded reader learns that while 30 per cent of the world's population consume 80 per cent of the entire produce of the earth, the remaining 70 per cent are left with only 20 per cent of its consumable goods. Six hundred and seventy million people are hungry, one billion do not have enough to eat on any day in their whole lives. Out of the 900 million children in the world, 600 million are hungry; 50 per cent of all children do not know the taste of milk. In India 50 per cent of the inhabitants die before they reach the age of 20. The average age of Middle Europeans lies between 65 and 70 years, while the average age of Indians is only 31.

The population is increasing at a speed never previously known—80,000 births per day. It is essential, therefore, to make provision at the same rate, for the necessary foodstuffs, clothing, living space, medical care, and opportunity for education and employment. In the meantime the world is lying in the grip of the cold war.

These alarming revelations have awakened public feeling—to the advantage of mankind, let us hope. "The aim of Christian solicitude, which occupies itself with mankind, is to make a workman out of a beggar": so ran the slogan at the Berlin Catholics' Day in 1958; and further: "It is the Christian aim to turn the hungry into healthy members of the human family." In November, 1959, too, the American bishops released a statement "On Freedom and Peace" in which they set forth the Christian principles which must govern the solving of the problems of the peoples of the world including that of their feeding.

But other conclusions have also been drawn from the alarming situation, and the demand has gone up vociferously: "Birth prevention by all methods! Limitation of births at any price!" Already some governments have legalized abortion, and in other countries efforts are being made to provide the people with "contraceptives."

These are measures with which as Christians we cannot agree, and we are in duty bound to make perfectly clear to the parties concerned in individual states and in international organizations that *there is a solution which is morally irreproachable*. It is not true that abortion and contraceptives are needed. We have only to make an effort if we wish to pursue the lawful way. One must be prepared for many severe struggles in respect to the moral aspect of the population problem.

As we are on the subject of healthy conformity with nature and orderly sexual activity, there is an aspect which demands a few serious words.

Into the civilized world of today, there has insinuated itself a poison against which an emphatic warning must be given. By this we mean those unnatural relations between persons of the same sex—homosexuality—for the social acceptance of which a campaign is being waged tenaciously and perseveringly in wide circles, especially in some countries of Western Europe.

Support for this is frequently based on the opinion of doctors who claim to have found that—besides the great number of persons normally constituted in respect of sex—there exists a small number of others, the "third sex," the balance of whose congenital qualities gives them a different sexual tendency because—so it is further claimed—their hormone distribution is in a proportion different from the normal.

Such a point of view is not tenable. It is a fact that a few people are born with malformations or organic disturbances in their hormone structure which also adversely affect their sex life. Such people require medical attention. Yet by far the greatest number of those who abandon themselves to unnatural practices are *in no way physically abnormal*. Rather they have been adversely affected by circumstances in their lives, such as defects in their education, evil influences in their environment, impressions or happenings which have disturbed their relations with the opposite sex, possibly to such an extent as to have given them a fear of marriage with its duties and of a family with its burdens.

In general, homosexuals do not differ from the rest of men in their nature but in their behavior. But this confers on them no right to an exceptional position. Their peculiarities are due to psychological disturbances which can be corrected.

It is a matter of experience that in dying civilizations and in periods of great upheaval the number of psychologically rootless and weak individuals always increases, and thus too the number of those who wish to acquire status through singularities. They simply want to be different, whether through esoteric thinking, decadence in art, eccentricity in their outward appearance and behavior, or through decadence in the exercise of their natural instincts.

Young, immature people, as might be expected, fall victim to the temptation to indulge in a variety of peculiarities. So long as this takes the form of a harmless rebellion against pretentiousness and the like, it may be regarded with an indulgent and understanding smile. But it is different when there arises the danger of a lapse in the domain of the sexual life. The rising generation must be vigilantly and effectively protected against all corruption and against every form of propaganda in favor of such dangerous and unnatural practices.

Moreover the cure is not to be found in exceptionally severe punishments, such as are, for example, provided by English law, and which can scarcely be looked upon as justified. No good purpose is achieved by such excesses.

3. Our debt of gratitude

Never before has mankind possessed the knowledge of the natural law through which since the beginning of time the Creator has regulated man's capacity to beget new life. In this twentieth century, two learned men, the Japanese doctor, Dr. Ogino, and the Austrian professor, Dr. Knaus, separately and independently discovered for the very first time the law of the periodic fertility and infertility in woman, implanted in nature by the Creator. It is a strange thing that this true and epoch-making discovery came to light just at the very period when the overpopulation of the earth threatens to become an alarming problem.

The believer likes to see in this a dispensation of divine Providence, for which we must be *grateful to the Creator*. On that account it is to be regretted that there is no lack of cavilers who have found fault with periodic abstinence in every way possible. Some claim that the reckoning of the days is an insult to the delicacy and the dignity of woman, others want to claim that this method is harmful to health.

This purely negative criticism is of very little value, for it is not possible to present to married couples, to all the millions of people who are seeking help, any other solution which is both efficient and morally irreproachable. This new knowledge stands essentially at the service of marriage and of its consolidation. Hence the effort to diffuse it as widely as possible is justified.

APPENDIX

CHART SHEET WITH
EXPLANATION AND EXAMPLE

How to use the Chart Sheet for women devised
by Dr. I. E. Georg

The Chart Sheets supplied on pp. 203–212 are a supplement to this book. Only those who have made themselves thoroughly conversant with the contents will be able to derive full advantage from the conscientious keeping of the Chart Sheet.

In Chapter IV, §2 and §3, the *cycle dates* and the *cycle phenomena* which ought to be noted are treated in considerable detail. If possible, also, the *waking temperature* should be noted daily; Chapters IV, §4 and VI, §4 c deal with this. Instead of the waking temperature, or in addition to it, the results of the *glucose test* may be noted. The glucose test is explained in great detail in Chapters II, §2 c, IV, §5 and VI, §4 c.

The Chart Sheet in question enables *all* these observations to be recorded on one single sheet simply, accurately, and in a form which is easy to read.

Four lines are provided for the recording of each individual cycle (see p. 202).

The first line: The date of the first day of the cycle goes in the left-hand column (cf. Chapter III, §2 a). All other noteworthy occurrences, except the temperature readings, should be recorded in the squares for the days of the cycle in question. Simple signs, symbolic letters, or shorthand may be used.

We recommend the use of the following symbols:

⌇⌇⌇(wavy line)	=	duration of menstruation
x	=	sexual intercourse
w	=	any unusually heavy work; exhaustion
c	=	change of climate, mountain climbing and the like
i	=	intermenstrual pain
o	=	ovulation
t	=	travel
(x)	=	severe emotional shock, fright, strong excitement

The second and third lines serve for marking in the waking temperature. The third line is prefixed by 97°; one records on this line, therefore, tenths of a degree from 97° up to 97.9° inclusively—for example, one records four-tenths for 97.4°. When the waking temperature rises to 98° or more, then one records the tenths (of degrees) on the second line which is prefixed by 98°.

On the *fourth line* the results of the glucose test are to be recorded.

The employment of the following abbreviations is recommended:

n	=	nil, no color	bb	=	bright blue, blue
lg	=	light green, green	db	=	dark blue
dg	=	dark green			

In order to avoid error and to ensure that the entries are placed in the right square, it is helpful to use the date-counting slide rule provided on the back jacket flap of this book. It is absolutely simple to use: the date (on the count rule) of the first day of the cycle is placed on the Chart Sheet, so that it actually corresponds with the square of the first day of the cycle (on the Chart Sheet). In this way, one can right away relate each further day of the cycle to its calendar date, or, conversely, one can easily read off which cycle day corresponds to a certain date. One need only observe how many days there are in the month in which the cycle began. The example supplied on p. 202 will clear up any obscurity which may yet remain.

The end of the cycle is marked by means of a heavy line after the last day of the cycle. If so desired, the wavy line which indicates menstruation can be added by way of further clarification. In order to discover which were the fertile and which the sterile days in the cycle just completed, and when ovulation probably took place, one counts the days back, as described in Chapter IV, §4. The use of the back-counting slide rule (also provided on the back jacket flap) will avoid error. This is placed on the cycle indications on the Chart Sheet so that two markings for the end of the cycle (on the Chart Sheet and on the rule) coincide. Then the limits of the fertile days (from the 12th to the 19th day before menstruation) are marked on the Chart Sheet with thick strokes; the day of ovulation can be marked O (15th day before menstruation).

The example given on p. 202 shows exactly how the rule for counting backward is used.

CHART SHEET according to Dr. I. E. Georg

For calculation of cycle days, marking in of rectal temperature and of glucose test

Date of first day of cycle	1	3	5	7	9	11	13	15	17	19	21	23	25	27	29	31	33	35	37	Exceptions
March 2				X X	X															
98°									0	X	1	0	0	X	0					
97°			4	5	4	6	5	2		1	0	2	2	1						
Glucose Test				4	6	5	5	7	6	3										
March 30				X X							1	2	0							
98°								1	2		1	2	1	1	2	0				
97°			3	6	5	5	4	2												
Glucose Test																				
April 27				X X						2	1	2			2	0				
98°			4	6	5	5	4	6	3	4	5	6	5	1						
97°									1	0	2									
Glucose Test																				
May 28				X X					1	0	2	1	2	0						
98°			3	5	6	5	6	5	2											
97°																				
Glucose Test																				

BACK COUNTING SLIDE RULE
designed by Dr. I. E. Georg

The fertile days of the cycle lie within the area outlined between 19th to 12th day before the start of the next menstruation. The greatest probability of conception exists on 17th, 16th, and 15th day before the start of menstruation.

Menstruation beginning of new cycle

Place here

Ovulation

DATE COUNTING SLIDE RULE
for use with Chart Sheet
Designed by Dr. I. E. Georg

Place here (20 on the first day of the cycle)

Jan., Feb., Apr., June, Aug., Sept., November	29 30 31
May, July, Oct., December	29 30 31
Mar. 1960, 64, 68 1972, 76, 80, 84	30 31
March when not Leap Year	31

When the new cycle starts on September 18 the previous cycle has lasted 29 days

CHART SHEET according to Dr. I. E. Georg for use with Date Counting Slide Rule and Back Counting Slide Rule

Date of first day of cycle	For calculation of cycle days, marking in of rectal temperature and of glucose test																			Exceptions
	1	3	5	7	9	11	13	15	17	19	21	23	25	27	29	31	33	35	37	
98°																				
97°																				
Glucose Test																				
98°																				
97°																				
Glucose Test																				
98°																				
97°																				
Glucose Test																				
98°																				
97°																				
Glucose Test																				
98°																				
97°																				
Glucose Test																				
98°																				
97°																				
Glucose Test																				
98°																				
97°																				
Glucose Test																				
98°																				
97°																				
Glucose Test																				
98°																				
97°																				
Glucose Test																				
98°																				
97°																				
Glucose Test																				
98°																				
97°																				
Glucose Test																				
98°																				
97°																				
Glucose Test																				
98°																				
97°																				
Glucose Test																				
Remarks																				
	2	4	6	8	10	12	14	16	18	20	22	24	26	28	30	32	34	36	38	

CHART SHEET according to Dr. I. E. Georg for use with Date Counting Slide Rule and Back Counting Slide Rule

Date of first day of cycle	For calculation of cycle days, marking in of rectal temperature and of glucose test																			
	1	3	5	7	9	11	13	15	17	19	21	23	25	27	29	31	33	35	37	Exception
98°																				
97°																				
Glucose Test																				
98°																				
97°																				
Glucose Test																				
98°																				
97°																				
Glucose Test																				
98°																				
97°																				
Glucose Test																				
98°																				
97°																				
Glucose Test																				
98°																				
97°																				
Glucose Test																				
98°																				
97°																				
Glucose Test																				
98°																				
97°																				
Glucose Test																				
98°																				
97°																				
Glucose Test																				
98°																				
97°																				
Glucose Test																				
98°																				
97°																				
Glucose Test																				
98°																				
97°																				
Glucose Test																				
98°																				
97°																				
Glucose Test																				
Remarks																				
	2	4	6	8	10	12	14	16	18	20	22	24	26	28	30	32	34	36	38	

204

CHART SHEET according to Dr. I. E. Georg for use with Date Counting Slide Rule and Back Counting Slide Rule

Date of first day of cycle	For calculation of cycle days, marking in of rectal temperature and of glucose test																			
	1	3	5	7	9	11	13	15	17	19	21	23	25	27	29	31	33	35	37	Exceptions
98° 97° Glucose Test																				
98° 97° Glucose Test																				
98° 97° Glucose Test																				
98° 97° Glucose Test																				
98° 97° Glucose Test																				
98° 97° Glucose Test																				
98° 97° Glucose Test																				
98° 97° Glucose Test																				
98° 97° Glucose Test																				
98° 97° Glucose Test																				
98° 97° Glucose Test																				
98° 97° Glucose Test																				
Remarks	2	4	6	8	10	12	14	16	18	20	22	24	26	28	30	32	34	36	38	

CHART SHEET according to Dr. I. E. Georg for use with Date Counting Slide Rule and Back Counting Slide Rule

Date of first day of cycle	For calculation of cycle days, marking in of rectal temperature and of glucose test																			Exceptions
	1	3	5	7	9	11	13	15	17	19	21	23	25	27	29	31	33	35	37	
98° 97° Glucose Test																				
98° 97° Glucose Test																				
98° 97° Glucose Test																				
98° 97° Glucose Test																				
98° 97° Glucose Test																				
98° 97° Glucose Test																				
98° 97° Glucose Test																				
98° 97° Glucose Test																				
98° 97° Glucose Test																				
98° 97° Glucose Test																				
98° 97° Glucose Test																				
98° 97° Glucose Test																				
98° 97° Glucose Test																				
Remarks	2	4	6	8	10	12	14	16	18	20	22	24	26	28	30	32	34	36	38	

206

CHART SHEET according to Dr. I. E. Georg for use with Date Counting Slide Rule and Back Counting Slide Rule

Date of first day of cycle	For calculation of cycle days, marking in of rectal temperature and of glucose test																			Exceptions
	1	3	5	7	9	11	13	15	17	19	21	23	25	27	29	31	33	35	37	
98° 97° Glucose Test																				
98° 97° Glucose Test																				
98° 97° Glucose Test																				
98° 97° Glucose Test																				
98° 97° Glucose Test																				
98° 97° Glucose Test																				
98° 97° Glucose Test																				
98° 97° Glucose Test																				
98° 97° Glucose Test																				
98° 97° Glucose Test																				
98° 97° Glucose Test																				
98° 97° Glucose Test																				
98° 97° Glucose Test Remarks																				
	2	4	6	8	10	12	14	16	18	20	22	24	26	28	30	32	34	36	38	

207

CHART SHEET according to Dr. I. E. Georg for use with Date Counting Slide Rule and Back Counting Slide Rule

Date of first day of cycle	For calculation of cycle days, marking in of rectal temperature and of glucose test																			
	1	3	5	7	9	11	13	15	17	19	21	23	25	27	29	31	33	35	37	Exception
98° 97° Glucose Test																				
98° 97° Glucose Test																				
98° 97° Glucose Test																				
98° 97° Glucose Test																				
98° 97° Glucose Test																				
98° 97° Glucose Test																				
98° 97° Glucose Test																				
98° 97° Glucose Test																				
98° 97° Glucose Test																				
98° 97° Glucose Test																				
98° 97° Glucose Test																				
98° 97° Glucose Test																				
98° 97° Glucose Test																				
Remarks	2	4	6	8	10	12	14	16	18	20	22	24	26	28	30	32	34	36	38	

208

CHART SHEET according to Dr. I. E. Georg for use with Date Counting Slide Rule and Back Counting Slide Rule

Date of first day of cycle	For calculation of cycle days, marking in of rectal temperature and of glucose test																			Exceptions
	1	3	5	7	9	11	13	15	17	19	21	23	25	27	29	31	33	35	37	
98°																				
97°																				
lucose Test																				
98°																				
97°																				
Glucose Test																				
98°																				
97°																				
Glucose Test																				
98°																				
97°																				
Glucose Test																				
98°																				
97°																				
Glucose Test																				
98°																				
97°																				
Glucose Test																				
98°																				
97°																				
ucose Test																				
98°																				
97°																				
ucose Test																				
98°																				
97°																				
ucose Test																				
98°																				
97°																				
ucose Test																				
98°																				
97°																				
ucose Test																				
98°																				
97°																				
ucose Test																				
98°																				
97°																				
ucose Test																				
Remarks																				
	2	4	6	8	10	12	14	16	18	20	22	24	26	28	30	32	34	36	38	

209

CHART SHEET according to Dr. I. E. Georg for use with Date Counting Slide Rule and Back Counting Slide Rule

Date of first day of cycle	For calculation of cycle days, marking in of rectal temperature and of glucose test																			
	1	3	5	7	9	11	13	15	17	19	21	23	25	27	29	31	33	35	37	Exceptions
98°																				
97°																				
Glucose Test																				
98°																				
97°																				
Glucose Test																				
98°																				
97°																				
Glucose Test																				
98°																				
97°																				
Glucose Test																				
98°																				
97°																				
Glucose Test																				
98°																				
97°																				
Glucose Test																				
98°																				
97°																				
Glucose Test																				
98°																				
97°																				
Glucose Test																				
98°																				
97°																				
Glucose Test																				
98°																				
97°																				
Glucose Test																				
98°																				
97°																				
Glucose Test																				
98°																				
97°																				
Glucose Test																				
Remarks																				
	2	4	6	8	10	12	14	16	18	20	22	24	26	28	30	32	34	36	38	

210

CHART SHEET according to Dr. I. E. Georg for use with Date Counting Slide Rule and Back Counting Slide Rule

Date of first day of cycle	For calculation of cycle days, marking in of rectal temperature and of glucose test																			Exceptions
	1	3	5	7	9	11	13	15	17	19	21	23	25	27	29	31	33	35	37	
98°																				
97°																				
Glucose Test																				
98°																				
97°																				
Glucose Test																				
98°																				
97°																				
Glucose Test																				
98°																				
97°																				
Glucose Test																				
98°																				
97°																				
Glucose Test																				
98°																				
97°																				
Glucose Test																				
98°																				
97°																				
Glucose Test																				
98°																				
97°																				
Glucose Test																				
98°																				
97°																				
Glucose Test																				
98°																				
97°																				
Glucose Test																				
98°																				
97°																				
Glucose Test																				
98°																				
97°																				
Glucose Test																				
Remarks																				
	2	4	6	8	10	12	14	16	18	20	22	24	26	28	30	32	34	36	38	

211

CHART SHEET according to Dr. I. E. Georg for use with Date Counting Slide Rule and Back Counting Slide Rule

Date of first day of cycle	For calculation of cycle days, marking in of rectal temperature and of glucose test																			
	1	3	5	7	9	11	13	15	17	19	21	23	25	27	29	31	33	35	37	Exception
98°																				
97°																				
Glucose Test																				
98°																				
97°																				
Glucose Test																				
98°																				
97°																				
Glucose Test																				
98°																				
97°																				
Glucose Test																				
98°																				
97°																				
Glucose Test																				
98°																				
97°																				
Glucose Test																				
98°																				
97°																				
Glucose Test																				
98°																				
97°																				
Glucose Test																				
98°																				
97°																				
Glucose Test																				
98°																				
97°																				
Glucose Test																				
98°																				
97°																				
Glucose Test																				
98°																				
97°																				
Glucose Test																				
98°																				
97°																				
Glucose Test																				
Remarks																				
	2	4	6	8	10	12	14	16	18	20	22	24	26	28	30	32	34	36	38	